architecture and computers

action and reaction in the digital design revolution

james steele

architecture and computers

action and reaction in the digital design revolution

Watson-Guptill Publications / New York

contents

introduction
the digital interface with hyper-reality: confronting an experimental architecture

06
70
120
136
158
206
224

THE DIGITAL INTERFACE WITH HYPER-REALITY: CONFRONTING AN EXPERIMENTAL ARCHITECTURE

The changes that the computer is bringing to architecture are one part of a revolutionary social upheaval that begs for brief discussion, to put the built component into context. This upheaval has been likened alternately to the Industrial Revolution, the introduction of movable type, the transfer to electricity, the invention of the telephone, the building of the railroad, or the switch to metal currency. As the world tries to cope with the vast implications of a change that far outdistances these precedents, and was largely unknown only five years ago, the realization is dawning that this is just the beginning; discussion about the Internet is minuscule compared to the pace of the change that is taking place. At the dawn of the twenty-first century, only about 40 percent of Americans are online, on slow telephone circuits. But Internet traffic is doubling every 95 days and about 2 million pages are added to the Web daily. There is almost three times as much e-mail sent as there is regular "snail" mail and, once broadband circuits are generally available, use is expected to increase exponentially due to the increased speed that is possible. What happens, a journalist has asked rhetorically, when "fast connections are ubiquitous rather than a luxury for a tiny minority? What happens once the Internet is always on, seamlessly built into our lives at home and at work, and all other media, from high quality video, to new forms yet to be seen, are instantly accessible through it?"[1] This cataclysmic change will have unforeseen impacts on all areas of public and private life, making previous social transformations seem minuscule by comparison, and making current debates about copyright, Internet pornography, and sites that proliferate political extremism irrelevant. Unlike previous upheavals, the Internet has had a magnified global impact, and promises to have a much greater one in the future, as it continues to reconfigure social, political, and cultural interaction all over the world. The nature of that reconfiguration is impossible to predict. All that is certain, based on past experience, is that this technology provides enormous potential for both good and bad.

A Puzzling Lack of Discussion about Digital Architecture

If the public debate about this potential, and the direction it may or should take has been relatively subdued, discussion about the implications for architecture has been especially muted. While some vocal critics, such as William Mitchell, have bravely stepped forward in an attempt to come to grips with this phenomenon and analyze possible outcomes, no manifestos have appeared to delineate a coherent vision of the drastic alterations to physical reality that are now underway. The epic grand debate that accompanied the Industrial Revolution, eloquently led by John Ruskin, William Morris, and Thomas Carlyle, changed the direction of architecture for the next century, even though none of these great Victorians was an architect. Peter Davey has convincingly argued that the idealism of the Arts and Crafts movement, which this debate engendered, transferred directly into early modernism, with only its theological overtones transformed by the secular character of production. No similar evolution may take place over the next century (or sooner, given the rapid pace of change) without such examination, which should be encouraged.

Blind Faith Mutes Debate

One reason for the silence may be the rapidity with which this electronic transformation has taken place; it is much more exciting and meaningful to participate in a revolution than to talk about it, but evidence of what has been characterized as "technological somnambulism" indicates a more profound phenomenon than that.[2] For all the supposed disenchantment with technology that is constantly described as having been experienced in the last half of the past century, due to nuclear proliferation, the inability to conquer pernicious diseases, global warming, general environmental degradation, and the theoretical end of a collective belief in the notion of progress, there is every indication that an implicit belief in progress is still alive and well, even if only at a subconscious level.

Polshek Partnership: Rose Center for Earth and Space (2000), New York
The computer has made new formal expression possible and these forms often
conform to the world view that it has inaugurated.

Toyo Ito: Mediatheque (2000), Sendai
Many architects are struggling with new ways to express
the potential of virtual space.

Japan is Having Second Thoughts

Blind faith in science is still intact, even in the face of the most sobering evidence to the contrary. Japan, for example, has been a paragon of a deeply ingrained belief in the saving grace of science, and a source of countless innovations during the last half of the twentieth century. Pride in its reputation as a leader in technology has allowed the nation to endure the humiliation of economic recession and unemployment that shattered the tacit paternal relationship between companies and their employees, who in the past were looked after for life in return for unquestioning loyalty. But a series of catastrophic accidents that occurred during a shaky recovery from the financial crisis caused a much more aggravated level of collective soul-searching, especially because they occurred in the nuclear, aerospace, and railway industries that were central to the Japanese self-image as world leaders in technology, and in which people had complete faith since they were repeatedly assured by government authorities that they were entirely safe.

The string of accidents began in June 1999, when a 400-pound (180-kilogram) section of concrete tunnel wall fell on a bullet train moving at 130 miles (210 kilometers) an hour, and four other collisions involving trains happened in quick succession in spite of assurances by the transport agency that inspectors did not detect loose concrete during maintenance checks. These were followed in September by the worst nuclear accident in Japanese history, caused when a fuel leak at a uranium processing plant in Tokaimura, Ibaraki Prefecture, left two workers in a critical condition and exposed more than 70 people to radiation. Government officials had also assured the public and especially nearby residents that such a leak could never occur.

Three months later, in early December, a Japanese space agency rocket with a government sponsored satellite on board crashed just after take-off, at a cost of $340 million. It was the second failure in two years for the H-2 rocket, which is the cornerstone of Japan's aspirations in the satellite launching market. A week after the crash China had no difficulty in launching its first rocket – designed as a prototype for carrying humans into orbit – and successfully brought it back to earth, joining the exclusive club of the United States and Russia in this category.

Self-flagellation at a level previously unthinkable in this proud nation swiftly followed; the head of the Ministry of Science and Technology resigned, a prominent professor at Tokyo University blamed the accidents on "a lack of responsibility and an arrogance on the part of engineers and industry," and the leading financial newspaper, the *Nikkei*, printed the headline "Japan's Big Technologies Start to Come Apart at the Seams" – sentiments echoed by the daily *Yomiuri*, which claimed that "Japan's Technology-Based State Becomes Shaky."[3]

While no-one believes that Japan's technological prowess has suffered a serious setback, this series of accidents has had a damaging effect on national self-image, already weakened by the awareness of the structural changes necessary in the social fabric, revealed by a severe economic recession. More than a critical loss of technological acuity, the sequence of failures has exposed a fundamental shift in cultural values, from an acceptance of labor-intensive jobs to a disdain for them among the younger generation. While the substance of Japan's scientific capability remains unchanged, the wide-spread image is now that of a country which has suffered a serious setback to its industrial and technological capability, the core of its miraculous economic recovery after the devastation of World War II.

NBBJ: Seoul Dome (1997–8)
Faith in technology continues to inspire much new design, in
spite of growing evidence that complete trust may be misplaced.

Normal Accident Theory Emerges

All this is not seen as purely coincidental by Charles Perrow, who formulated his "normal accident theory" in the early 1980s to account for the increasing frequency of such catastrophes. His book *Normal Accidents: Living With High Risk Technologies* (1984) is based on the premise that the organizations now responsible for such complex contemporary technologies are so "tightly integrated that accidents are inevitable, or 'normal', even when all the proper safety procedures are followed." [4] He cites disasters such as the meltdown of the nuclear reactor at Three Mile Island in Pennsylvania and the explosion of the Space Shuttle Challenger as a normal consequence of the intricacy of the systems themselves rather than human error. Perrow would argue that even though the leak at the Tokaimura nuclear plant was caused when technicians poured nearly seven times the allowable amount of uranium into a purification tank, resulting in an explosion, and that the JCO Company, which operates the plant, has been accused in the local news media of failing to instruct staff of the danger of using too much uranium during the manufacturing process, the complexity of the system itself made such an accident inevitable. Bolstered by a shocking report, published in late December 1999 by the American National Academy of Sciences, which recounts how more people are killed each year by lethal medical accidents than by AIDS in the United States, and by the embarrassing disappearance of the Mars Polar Lander as the latest expensive

miscalculation by NASA, researchers in areas as diverse as social science and finance have appropriated normal accident theory from engineering in an attempt to identify potential disasters in their fields.

Comparisons have been made between normal accident and high-reliability theory. But normal accident advocates are far more skeptical about the risks posed by the back-up systems that high-reliability analysts cite as evidence of safety. Normal accident theorists believe that redundancy just adds another layer of complexity, increasing danger. They also make more of the technological-political link, believing that only vested interest promotes safety.

Technological Determinism Precludes Debate

Consensual complicity in the suppressed hope that technology really is capable of satisfying all physical and emotional needs – in spite of overwhelming evidence to the contrary – may explain the complete absence of debate, and the violent reaction against disbelief on the rare occasions that it does occur. The prevailing attitude about the increasing reliance on computers during the design process, as part of the electronic revolution just described, is that the technology is beyond question and above discussion. The future it promises to shape is formulated as infinitely desirable, inevitable, and improved. [5]

Technological determinism, predicated on the belief that social benefit is entirely dependent on scientific discovery, focuses on innovation rather

than the consequences. A recent full-page advertisement in the *New York Times*, placed by a well known investment firm that has profited from Internet sales, proves the syndrome is alive and well:

We love technology. It's new and it's shiny and it inspires a certain awe, like the Great Pyramid of Cheops or a tiny new human being. Technology is good at the heavy lifting. People are good at the heavy thinking. Bits and bytes and ones and zeros fly around the planet, but only at our discretion. The computer has a role model, and it is us. Computers are plastic and metal and sand. People are brilliance and discernment and vision. Admire machines. Worship their inventors. [6]

The assumptions embodied in this seemingly innocuous, disturbingly heretical advertisement – that technology is a neutral force that we can control, and that this equation will always balance – has generated debate which has a direct bearing on the possible future of computers in architecture.

**Coop Himmelb(l)au: UFA Cinema
(1993–8), Dresden**
Nature has often been relegated to scenography in favor
of phantasmagorical, internalized worlds.

The New Luddites

A new breed of Luddites, who are establishing
a cult following but are hardly a household word,
differ from the original rebels at the start of the
Industrial Revolution in their thorough knowledge
and use of the technology they conspire against;
they uniformly agree on its advantages, but warn
of unconditional acceptance. Prominent among
these, in the United States, are Hubert L. Dreyfus
of the University of California at Berkeley; Joseph
Weizenbaum, now retired from the Massachusetts
Institute of Technology; Albert Borgmann at the
University of Montana; Richard E. Sclove, founder
of the Loka Institute in Amherst, Massachusetts;
Gary Chapman, director of the Twenty-first Century
Project at the Lyndon B. Johnson School of Public
Affairs at the University of Texas at Austin;
Langdon Winner, Professor at Rensselaer
Polytechnic Institute in New York; Andrew Light,
Assistant Professor at the State University of New
York at Birmingham; Stephen L. Talbott, author
of *The Future Does Not Compute: Transcending
the Machines in Our Midst*, and editor of a small
but influential e-mail newsletter *NetFuture* (which
counts among its 5,000 or so subscribers many
people involved with the Internet as well as
nationally recognized computer scientists); and
Clifford Stoll, author of *Silicon Valley Snake Oil*.

Three Avatars of Limits

Of these, Hubert Dreyfus, Joseph Weizenbaum,
and Albert Borgmann have the highest seniority,
having each been appraising computer technology
for more than 25 years. Dr. Dreyfus first registered
his doubts in 1972 with the publication of *What
Computers Can't Do: A Critique of Artificial
Reason*, followed by *What Computers Still Can't Do*
a decade later. Primarily written in response to the
rapidly growing enthusiasm for artificial intelligence
in the early 1970s, the first book is divided into
roughly five parts. The first traces the construction
of the belief in value-free science, beginning with
the Platonic separation of knowledge from belief
and the distrust of intuition, through the firm
grounding of the rationalist tradition by Gottfried
Leibnitz in his attempt to reduce the material world
to calculation and all knowledge to a deductive
system, and by Thomas Hobbes, who stressed the
syntactic connection between thought and
calculation and the central role that reason plays
as the essence of being human.

Following this overview of how rationality came
to dominate Western scientific tradition, Dreyfus
recounts how the computer evolved, beginning
with the "Analytic Engine" first devised by Charles
Babbage in Britain in 1835 – basically a digital
computer run by punch cards. Dreyfus finds great
significance in the fact that this first effort was
digital, describing in great detail the difference
between this representation of quantities by
discrete states – in which relays are either open
or closed in one of ten positions – and the analog
measurement of physical quantities. He then
describes how digitization really only became
practical after the telephone was introduced, using
H.H. Aiken's electromechanical digital computer
(which used 3,000 telephone relays in 1944) as
an example. This project was based on Leibniz's
belief that all thought has universal characteristics
that allow it to be reduced to abstract symbols,
and that any thought process can be formalized
and represented as a series of instructions to be
replicated by discrete elements. His history of
the computer continues with a discussion of the
pioneering work of A.M. Turing in the early 1950s,
the development of information theory by Claude E.
Shannon, the comparison of heuristic and
algorithmic programmes by Herbert Simon and
Allen Newell in the 1950s, and the contribution
of Anthony Oettinger, who simulated simple
conditioning and practical intelligence and sought
to use a computer to associate words and objects
in 1952, driven by a belief that it could be
programmed "to understand the essence of
human reason."[7]

After an extensive third section, which details
the two phases of Artificial Intelligence
distinguishable at the time of the publication of
his book, along with a lengthy documentation of
their failures, Dreyfus establishes four basic
assumptions as the book's fourth section and
general conclusions as a fifth, each of which has
specific relevance in the use of computers in
architectural design today.[8] Breaking down the
expectations of program designers into categories,
he characterizes the first of these as the biological
assumption that the human neural net can be
simulated. He claims that is a fallacy, that the
neural switch model of the brain is untenable

because it is not heuristic. The brain functions more like an analog than digital computer, with thoughts being irreducible to symbols in a descriptive language in which each carries a specific bit of information, having instead "volleys of pulses" which cannot be correlated into steps in an information processing sequence.[9] In the analog computer physical variables represent the information being processed, mimicking the rate of pulses in the brain, where presynaptic barrages are algebraically graded according to synaptic potential and then directed to a pathway depending on their value.

Distinguishing between physical processes and consciousness, Dreyfus then identifies the second, psychological assumption that psychology, as the science of human behavior, advances theories which provide understanding of why certain kinds of behavior occur, and that these are then confused with explanations of how behavior is produced in attempts to digitize them. Arguing that information is not meaning, Dreyfus emphasizes that while physiochemical processes can be formulated and calculated discretely, it does not mean that discrete processes are taking place. Simulation does not equal representation; the mind subtly distinguishes between relevant and irrelevant information in an empirical process. The third assumption he identifies, the epistemological fallacy, involves a subtle distinction from the psychological, since it also involves the assumption that intelligent behavior can be formalized into instructions for a digital computer. The difference

is that the psychological assumption is based on the belief that the rules used to formalize behavior can be used to produce or reproduce it, while the epistemological assumption specifies that only non-arbitrary behavior can be formalized and reproduced. This is a hold-over from the assertion by Plato in *Euthyphro* that only non-arbitrary actions have a rational structure, which can be expressed in a theory or set of rules which implicitly follows. In rebuttal, Dreyfus cites Ludwig Wittgenstein, arguing that people do not always act rationally, and that intentions and interpretations differ. The fourth and final position Dreyfus identifies is the ontological assumption that everything essential to intelligent behavior must be understandable in terms of a set of deterministic, independent elements, which in his opinion does not account for the human capacity for fringe consciousness and the ability to tolerate ambiguity while processing information, to discriminate between essential and inessential details, and to group them "perspicuously."

He concludes by asserting that each of these four assumptions is axiomatic, assuming that a human being is a device that operates according to rules, and is reinforced by a 2,000-year-old rationalistic tradition that can be traced back to the Platonic reduction of all reasoning to rules, without taking interpretation into account. He cites an equally well established philosophical tradition, proposing a different phenomenological description of the structure of human behavior legible in the work of Martin Heidegger, Wittgenstein, Maurice

Merleau-Ponty, Michael Polanyi, Charles Taylor, and Samuel Todes, who argue for the indeterminacy of human perception, and the significance of corporal experience in decision making.[10]

Technology is Not Neutral

Rather than attacking the fallacies inherent in assuming that a computer can model human reason and behavior, Joseph Weizenbaum, and to some extent Albert Borgmann, the other two avatars calling for a more measured approach to this technology, focus on its power to usurp our ability to act independently, as well as the tendency to substitute information for reality. They stress that far from being neutral, technology and the tools it provides reshape the tasks it is used for, as well as the meaning of those tasks and the characteristics of its users. Recent research on the early implementation of tools indicates that they played a much more important role in human evolution than previously realized; when prehuman arthropods first used tools their physical condition changed as their dexterity increased. It was the success of the most rudimentary tools that triggered human evolution and that can account for evolution's relative speed. In their realization that biological evolution is quickly giving way to a technological equivalent, the question anthropologists now ask is: can a machine be more intelligent than its maker? Advertising assurances aside, the answer is an unqualified yes.[11]

Tools not only change individual patterns and behavior, but also cause transformations in the

Hamzah and Yeang: Nagoya 2006 Tower
Structural innovation has been prompted by digital transformations,
changing the skylines of cities around the world.

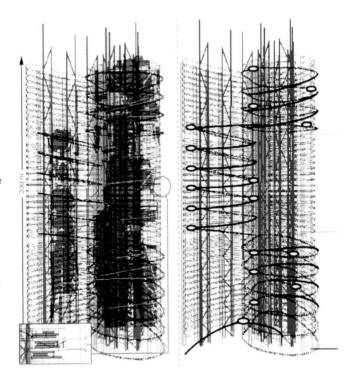

institutions that are the social analogy of these
personal habits. Technology profoundly affects
the cultural, political, and psychological conditions
of a society and is reciprocally shaped by
socioeconomic forces. The ancient, internalized,
kinesthetic connection between tools and their
makers, in which they become both physical and
psychological extensions of their users, may
also partially explain the lack of reflection and
discussion about the possible consequences of the
use of the computer in design. Just as other tools
have in the past, the computer is in the process
of conditioning our understanding of the world and
our perception of our place in it. It is more than a
pragmatic means to an end, or an inert piece of
plastic and metal, it is a virtual constituent in a very
real and symbolic reconstruction of the world that
is now underway. It is also the most powerful
manifestation yet of the human ability to use
technology to subdue nature.[12] In addition to
shaping behavior, technology always generates
unanticipated environmental and social
consequences, and qualifies as a social structure
because it affects politics and culture, regulates
social behavior through subtle coercion,
reconfigures prior patterns, and hinders or
transforms other technologies. It also affects
people peripheral to it, exerts a symbolic influence
on society, reconfigures opportunities, transforms
individual and collective psychological development,
and redirects authoritarian processes which
become binding on individuals and groups.[13]

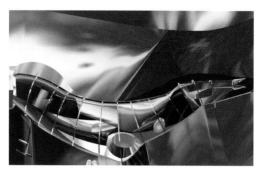

NOX: H₂O Expo water pavilion, Zeeland, the Netherlands
By letting the computer take the lead, some designers have opened the door for an evolutionary design process.

Le Corbusier: Millowner's headquarters (1954), Ahmedabad
The blind belief in progress implicit in High Modernism – epitomized by the later work of Le Corbusier – continues unabated in cyberspace.

Techno-Erotic Seduction

Another reason for the compelling appeal of the computer is its subliminal sexiness at a time when physical sex has been suppressed by the real fear of death that may accompany it. This techno-erotic quality of the computer is partially implicit in the replacement of machines of production with what Frederic Jamison has termed "machines of reproduction"; the invisible metamorphosis from sensual machined object to erotic virtual image that has occurred in the transition from the industrial to the information age.[14]

The machine age equivalent of the erotic images provided by the computer are Le Corbusier's references to grain silos, ships, airplanes, trains, and automobiles in *Vers Une Architecture*, as well as by the Futurists' paeans to speed in their manifestos that appeared at the same time. But unlike the conscious gendering of the objects of industrial desire, such as the ship, which was always referred to as feminine, the computer is significantly to be androgynous. *Crash*, the 1973 novel by J.G. Ballard which caused so much controversy in its film version, confronts this transition directly. The not-so-subliminal message behind the disturbing images of a sado-masochistic obsession with speed and the pain that it can cause, which many found to be so offensive, is the close relationship between technology, sexuality, and death. The critical link between the sensual objects of machine production that Ballard and Le Corbusier revelled in and the detached eroticism of the "machines of

reproduction" is well established in Platonic metaphysics. In trying to explain the differences inherent in cyberspace, Michael Heim refers to Plato's *Symposium*, in which Dioturia, the priestess of love, describes the proportional relationship between eroticism and spirituality, between physical and mental stimulation. She equates evolutionary, biological imperatives with mental desire and the psychological need to increase knowledge. "On the primal level," Heim explains, "Eros is a drive to extend our finite being, to prolong something of our physical selves beyond our mortal existence."[15]

Mental Desire Consummated in Digital Intercourse

Ideas, in this physical-mental intercourse, become like children, born from the psyche as formalized perceptions which develop a heightened awareness in both their parents and those who experience and fully understand them. Perhaps this is why an idea, finally developed as far as a presentation to a client, often seems as real to an architect as a finished building. This consciousness is certainly amplified in virtual space, where entities are more clearly described and defined, and the viewer more thoroughly immersed in them. Heim explains that the word matrix – the "bright lattices of logic unfolding across a colorless void" evoked in the novel *Neuromancer*, where William Gibson first introduced the word cyberspace – stems from the Latin word for mother, confirming its generative-erotic origins and "connecting the Platonic concept of ideal form to the information systems of today."[16]

NOX: Beachness, Noordwijk
Contextual elements, such as the reflection of sunlight, were once difficult to factor into building designs, but now they can actually generate form.

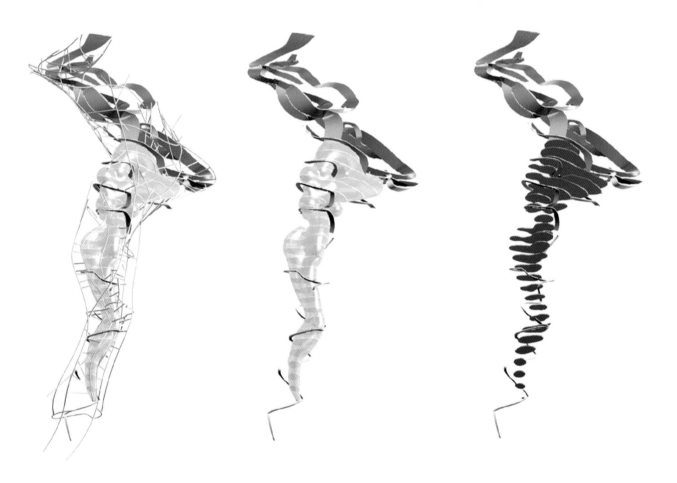

Polshek Partnership: Rose Center for Earth and Space
The perception that the world is shrinking, encouraged by the
Internet, is reflected in much new design.

Perfect Forms Realized in Cyberspace

In this connection between Eros and Logos, logic redirects love to perfect forms. The perfect geometric solids and ideal numbers that Plato associated with intellectual, reliable truth rather than its deceptive sensory equivalent, are finally realized and empirically defined in cyberspace. Pure cognition is compromised by digital re-creations derived from stored data, which is derived externally. The Platonic dream, of a crystal clear vision of reality seen through a mental rather than physical eye, is replaced by an existential construct, a reality reconstituted from information, constrained by binary choice. The computer simulates the body, embodies personality; the perception that it sometimes anticipates commands and has become an extension of the body is symptomatic of this simulation.

A New Space-Time Relationship

The radical change that has taken place in architectural conception has occurred at the most substantive level of space, the intangible medium with which the architect has been the most familiar, the manipulation and thoughtful making of which has distinguished the profession from the more pragmatic discipline of building. The computer has precipitated a fundamental re-evaluation of space and time, the transition from a pre-industrial condition to cyberspace taking place in about a century. If the ancient perception of time was cyclical and diurnal, its connection to space was considered to be subjective and absolute, as

ongoing research on the relationship between Stonehenge and the landforms around it, for example, are beginning to demonstrate. Such monuments, up to and including the Gothic cathedrals of the Middle Ages, were communal projects built over generations.[17] With the advent of clock time, tied to production, the pairing of space and time became sequential, objective, and rapidly relative. Einstein showed in his theory of relativity that space and time are aspects of the same entity, posited the space-time continuum, and explained that three-dimensional space is perceived differently, depending on speed and point of view.

Modern, Post-modern, and Digital Space Briefly Reconsidered

In relationship to architecture, the social fragmentation precipitated by the Industrial Revolution — and the rural-urban migration that accompanied it — prompted modern simplification. The stripped-down interiors produced by Charles Rennie Mackintosh and Margaret McDonald were part of a rapidly consolidating Arts and Crafts tradition that emerged in response to mechanization, but were also inspired by the Zen reductivism of Japan, an ultratraditional culture that was just then beginning to open up to the world. Their direct assimilation of Japanese ideas of proportion and restraint was often echoed in the early phase of the Modern Movement that followed, and which was in no small way set in a certain trajectory by them.[18] Once the initiative — partially relinquished by those who failed to recognize the value of the contribution

**Richard Meier: Getty Center
(1984–97), Los Angeles**
Prominent examples of Late Modernism extend the debate
about the place of nature in the public realm.

**Bernard Tschumi: Parc de la Villette
(1984–90), Paris**
During its short ascendancy, Deconstruction reinforced
technological determinism, proclaiming that machines
had displaced nature.

being made by Mackintosh and McDonald –
crossed the English Channel, an important insight
by Adolf Loos further refined this reductivism.
The missionary zeal for cleaning up the clutter of
the Victorian drawing-room fattened by the profits
of production, which had been formalized by the
Arts and Crafts movement, was reconfigured to
accommodate the monadism that became a central
feature of the modern experience, captured by
Edvard Munch in his painting of 1893, *The Scream*.

Loos saw the need to soften Mackintosh and
McDonald's call for minimalism, since the traditional
culture that inspired it still had the benefit of
pre-industrial communal support, and the need for
reductivism came from a response to economies
of scale rather than to excess. Instead, he
substituted the realization of the exterior as an
anonymous façade masking a sheltering interior
space, a final personal refuge from a newly hostile
world outside. [19] Rather than re-instituting clutter,
however, Loos replaced white surfaces with luxury
materials such as leather and marble and a
Raumplan reminiscent, but not a literal replicant, of
traditional room divisions to create a spatial haven
that was to be the antidote for the loneliness of
a market-driven world, the final internal repository
of individual history and culture.

While Mies van der Rohe perpetuated the
Loosian ideal of internal luxury best expressed in
its apotheosis at the Barcelona Pavilion, he did
away with the *Raumplan*, and Le Corbusier's
subsequent return to extreme minimalism on both
the exterior and interior left the individual no place
to hide. This reductivist, space-positive pattern was
subsequently reproduced thoughtlessly by many
less talented practioners, and reproduced more
thoughtfully by some, such as the New York Five in
the Sixties, who thought through Le Corbusier's
Five Points, reproduced them in variants, and took
them seriously as an intellectual as well as a
physical exercise. Some late-twentieth-century
examples, such as the Getty Museum in Los
Angeles by Richard Meier, show the durability of
the modernist, space-positive approach, with a
teleological world view that is evident in its
processional sequences. The building displaces
pre-industrial spirituality with a structurally ordered
reproduction of scientific rationalism, as a rival to
religion in providing meaning in the world. The
interior spaces that this structure makes possible –
and through which this procession is planned for
maximum effect – is the grand narrative in
microcosm, revealed by natural light, a tectonic
explanation of a universal history of belief in
progress and a break with the past. Modernization
is a process of cultural differentiation and social
atomization, due to the fragmentation of the pre-
industrial community and so defines modernism as
the built equivalent of this process. [20]

Post-modern Space

Proof that modernity is an incomplete project lies in the permutation of architectural space – from modernism through post-modernism – into cyberspace in which the search for continuities is more productive than an obsession with disjunctions. The unifying thread, as Frederic Jamison has pointed out, is capitalism, with the rapid growth of consumerism and an increasing awareness of the difficulties that parallel the advantages of technology, such as that now occurring in Japan, defining each phase. Post-modernism began as a questioning of the possible limits of the process of modernization, rather than a refutation of it.[21] The proliferation of a global economy and the advent of the post-industrial society have helped bring about the multiculturalism that has ended the differentiation and elitism of modernism, and the media explosion that has accompanied it has undermined perceptions of social stability and fixed institutional structures, including a reliance on specialization. This promotion of "heterogeneity without hierarchy" emerges in its built equivalent, as does the realization of the end of the grand narrative, the idea that there is one answer to all the problems in the world, replaced by skepticism and multivocality.[22]

Jamison contends that there are serious doubts about the concept of progress, stating that the beginning of the end of the grand narrative began earlier in the twentieth century, after the end of World War I, and he has made four key points about the relationship between modernity and post-modernity. These are that: (1) consumer cycles now force us to "periodize" because we are conditioned to do so, and these cycles encourage the reconsideration of modernism from the vantage point of post-modernity; (2) modernity is a "narrative" category which implies premodern, unmodern, and post-modern equivalents; (3) modernity is a process of separation that begins with a dichotomy between subject and object; and (4) any consideration of modernity must involve post-modernity, since both are stages in the growing artificiality of consumer culture.[23]

Post-modern Space Reinvented as a Tangible Cybernetic Equivalent

To further put the imminent journey into cyberspace into perspective, it helps to briefly recall the discussion about post-modern space as a product of the growing trend toward mass consumption prompted by the media and advertising from the middle of the twentieth century. As the dimensional equivalent of the differentiation that was then beginning to erode the boundaries of class, educational background and the notion of taste that informed modernist space, post-modern space instead represented a hierarchy based on consumption. It was a reaction to the erosion of fixed social structures, stable boundaries, and hierarchies that had characterized the first half of the twentieth century. Described as being heterogeneous without hierarchy, this space reflected the destruction of the belief in expertise and specialization previously manifested in compartmentalized, functionalist boxes.

Sociologists, planners, and geographers insist that the post-modern condition continues and if so, its architectural equivalent today surely must be Theming, a phenomenon begun in earnest by Walt Disney. It is no coincidence that thematic and digital architecture are proliferating at the same rate. There is a direct correlation between virtual experience and its themed environment, especially at the level of the sensual and erotic distinction discussed earlier, which makes comparison useful.

Cyberspace, Cybertime

The advent of virtual reality has made it difficult to consider reality in the same way; it has irrevocably altered perceptions of the everyday world of space and time. The circular, rather than sequential, order of time caused by the retrieval of information as well as the variation between the sense of protracted time, and what Paul Virilio has called "intensive" time in cyberspace, has contributed to what he has also referred to as a corresponding "morphological breakdown in the dimensional field."[24] Intriguingly, this corresponds to recent progress in quantum mechanics, in which efforts to unify gravity have led to the introduction of a concept of "imaginary" time, completely coterminous with all directions in space, as an abstract scientific law. The accompanying realization is that in "real" time there is an important difference between direction, past, and future. This difference is dictated by the second law of thermodynamics, which predicts that in any closed system entropy (the measure of disorder in that system) increases with time, which implies direction.[25] This direction

Michael Graves: Clos Pegase Winery (1987), Napa Valley
The failure of Post-modernism to re-establish a humanistic basis in
architecture has given the technological imperative precedence by default.

Polshek Partnership:
Rose Center for Earth and Space
The vision of a brave new world must be
tempered by a realistic assessment of limitations.

has been designated by physicists as "the arrow of time." The "arrow of time", aside from entropic progression, also includes a psychological direction, in which we perceive that time passes, and a cosmological direction, in which the universe has been expanding since the Big Bang occurred, between 5 and 10 percent every thousand million years. Theories of quantum mechanics developed in the study of black holes have also refined an understanding of space; particle theory has shown that there is no such thing as empty space, because gravitational and electromagnetic fields would have to have a value of zero for this to be the case. Quantum fluctuations in the values of these fields have indicated the existence of pairs of particles that are not "real," since they cannot be measured directly with a particle detector, but have been classified as "virtual," because their indirect effects can be measured and predicted theoretically. [26]

Definitions of Cyberspace

Several working definitions of cyberspace have been proposed, one of the most inclusive by Michael Benedict, who has written extensively on the subject. Benedict defines cyberspace as "a globally networked, computer-sustained, computer-accessed and computer-generated, multidimensional, artificial or 'virtual' reality," but adds to that carefully circumscribed explanation with a more lyrical, almost anthropomorphic description of it as blooming "wherever data gathers and is stored. Its depths increase with every image or word or number, with every addition, every contribution, of fact or thought. Its horizons recede in every direction; it breathes larger, it complexifies, it embraces and invalues. Billowing, glittering, humming, coursing, a Borgesian library, a city, intimate, immense, firm, liquid, recognizable and unrecognizable at once." [27]

His definition conjures up the image of a parallel universe created and sustained by computers, a place without boundaries that can be accessed by anyone, anywhere, who has the technology, an evocation of the perfect metaphysical realm described by Plato, not bounded by the same physical laws and geometrical restraints as this world. The not-so-potent anthropomorphism presupposes objective regard of information, implying total synthesis with it instead. We become the information, and this projection of ourselves into the totality of this sensory world is much of the reason for its seductive appeal. The computer simulates the body and like the best of tools, seems to anticipate its needs, and even the personality of the user. Cyber is derived from the Greek word *kyberman* ("to steer or control") and this is perhaps its ultimate appeal for architects, whose basic impulse to control is very strong − in spite of remonstrations to the contrary. The exhilaration that goes with feeling in control of information is immediate, if deceptive, since predictions are that the computer will end up in control.

Peter Eisenman: Staten Island Institute Center for Electronic Culture, New York
Contextual information is now being programmed into the design process to ensure a
connection between architecture and its surroundings.

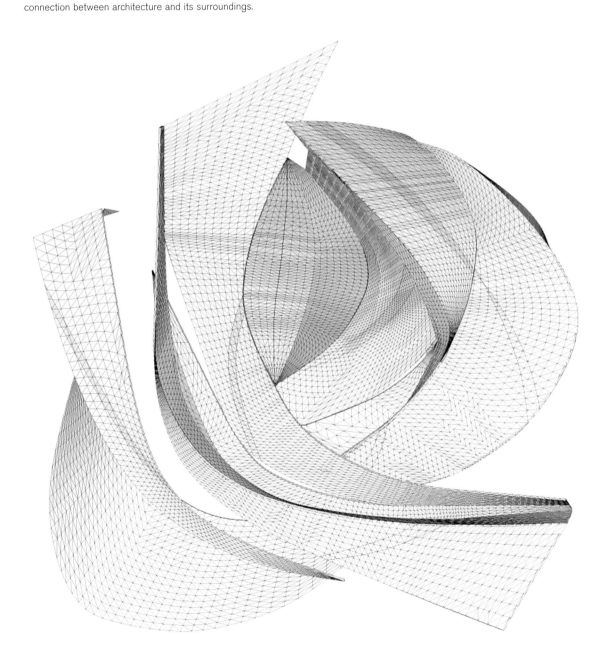

Polshek Partnership:
Civic Center Music Hall, Oklahoma City
Exploding components of a structure makes spatial relationships clearer.

Polshek Partnership:
Civic Center Music Hall, Oklahoma City
While aesthetically beguiling, new color palettes are also misleading when compared to the built result.

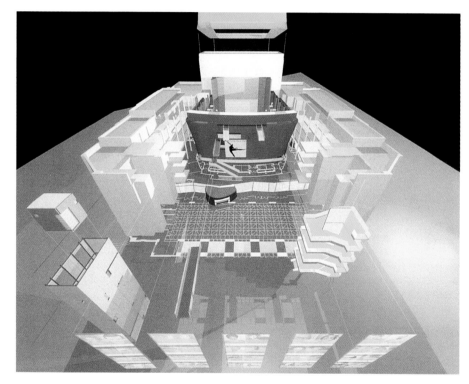

A Critique

The issues involved in architecture generated in the multi-dimensional "virtual" reality of cyberspace must begin with space itself. The counterpoint to the abstract, experimental modulation of virtual space now underway is the ongoing phenomenological investigation of the "real" world from the viewpoint of ethnicity, politics, economics and gender, as well as the far more comprehensive "science of space" proposed by Henri Lefebvre and the detailed examination of the connection between human perception and spatial values by Maurice Merleau-Ponty. Such investigations are at the forefront of the new cultural politics of difference, the debate between the defenders of digital and diverse space distinguished by what Cornel West has described as the desire to eliminate. "The monolithic and homogeneous in the name of diversity, multiplicity and heterogeneity; to reject the abstract, general and universal in light of the concrete, specific and particular, and to historicize, contexturalize and pluralize by highlighting the contingent, provisional, variable, tentative, shifting and changing…"[28] This desire is manifest in the important way in which issues such as extremism, empire, class, race, gender, sexual orientation, age, nationality, and history are now treated differently among social critics of all disciplines. Virtual reconstruction may be considered counter-representational to this new ontology, precluding or negating it, since it undermines our fundamental, intentional relationship with reality. Reality, as Paul Virilio has observed, "is always generated, never given; it is built by the way a society develops, by the way a society learns. Each reality is followed by another. We are living in a degenerate reality, a reality of the moment. It is a matter of the virtual regenerating the real."[29]

As the phenomenologists labor to uncover and represent cultural and individual difference, the increasing onslaught of information today has an opposite effect. This information is structural but not differentiated, the priorities necessary to establish meaning are as difficult to distinguish as the difference between the "real" present and the way it is represented in the media. Digital conversion involves judgment and selection by someone other than the ultimate users or recipients of the information involved, who tacitly relinquish their right to differentiate between cultures, geographical locations, relationships, and individuals by accepting this preselection.[30]

Space with Texture

Henri Lefebvre is one of the most comprehensive cultural detectives searching out difference today. His landmark work, *The Production of Space*, first appeared in French in 1974, was translated into English in 1991, and is still in print. He epitomizes the chasm that exists between the substantive examinations of space now being undertaken by critical geographers and the textural abstraction of its virtual equivalent. Lefebvre has been one of the first to theorize extensively about the spatial implications of the categories of difference that Cornel West has enumerated, superseding studies of the way power is contextualized by critics such as Michel Foucault by expanding the argument to an international scale in parallel with the phenomenon of globalization. He admittedly has an agenda – stated late in his *avant-projet* but constantly legible between the lines – of advancing the "meta-Marxist critique of the representations of power" to include the spaces of everyday life as the new arena where the struggle for control is enacted; instead of just focusing on the workplace or in the obvious places where surveillance is carried out by the state, such as prisons. Arguing convincingly that the global geography of capitalism has substantially changed, he attempts to construct a hypothesis of space that includes developing and developed nations alike to contradict the homogenizing effects of globalization. His "strategic" hypothesis is that "theoretical and practical questions relating to space are becoming more and more important. These questions, though they do not suppress them, tend to resituate concepts and problems having to do with biological reproduction, and with the production both of the means of production themselves and of consumer goods."[31] Far from being an objective rational proposal, however, this hypothesis is intended to be catalytic and confrontational, a proactive, life-changing framework in sharp contrast to the critical theories it is intended to replace, which Lefebvre dismisses as passé.

Abstract or Virtual Space

In spite of its clearly articulated political agenda, Lefebvre's ontology may be usefully appropriated in an objective discussion about virtual space, which may arguably be considered a product of what he characterizes as abstract space. Prior to his study, he notes that the word "space" was usually associated with Euclidean geometry, or was considered to be infinite, empty ether. His introduction of the concept of "social" space had to compete with the epistemological convention of space as a mental place, widely generalized into literary, ideological, psychoanalytic, or other variations that excluded a more uniformly humanistic point of view. He sought to bridge this "abyss" between the mental concept of space then being described by philosophers and epistemologists and the real, physical implications of its social equivalent. This bridge consisted of nothing less than a "science of space" that he hoped would lead to a more thorough knowledge of it by representing the social relationships of the "neocapitalist" forces of production, the ideology concealed by those forces, and the possibilities inherent in the real framework he uncovered. Proposing that the idea that economics and capitalism pragmatically influence space – from building construction through investment and the division of labor – is a commonplace, he nonetheless offers a reminder of the various kinds of capitalism operating today, including multinationals, international banks, and other financial and governmental agencies, and of the

hegemony that these systems wield over institutions and ideas. He emphasizes that hegemony, especially in relationship to space, is maintained by one class "by all available means, and knowledge is one such means. The connection between knowledge (savoir) and power is thus made manifest." [32]

Lefebvre seeks, in his "science of space," to construct a unitary theory that would interweave previously existing mental maps, including formal and logical explanations, with physical, natural, or cosmological fields and his own primary interest of social space, including specializations of architecture and urban planning. He is aware of the potential of such a theory to gloss over important differences in each of these areas and seeks to allow polemics to emerge. Considering the relationship of the natural sciences to space, he rejects the "arrow of time" concept, previously mentioned in connection with the Big Bang theory, preferring instead to subscribe to a cosmology based on a universe made up of a multiplicity of particular spaces that are the product of energy. He effectively derails the causality and teleology that are implicit in the more widely accepted arrow of time model. [33] He also rejects literary descriptions of space, especially in urban experience, as being too general to be useful – in spite of inspired contributions such as those of Quatremère de Quincy and Victor Hugo – and settles instead on Hegel's "concrete universal" as a starting point in his search for a generative mechanism to replace the prevailing philosophical

view of space as a static mental construct. He calls this mechanism "production," which, intentionally or not, has connotations of manufacture, and its fabrication goes far beyond discourse to provide a code that brings "the various kinds of space and the modalities of their genesis together within a single theory." Rather than emphasizing the formal aspect of codes, he stresses their "dialectical" character as part of a practical relationship, or "interaction between 'subjects' and their space and surroundings." [34] His realization of these codes, and acknowledgement of their "coming into being and disappearance," conforms to the "realities" mentioned earlier by Paul Virilio, which change as each society develops.

The Hegelian fulcrum allows Lefebvre to examine the role of history in the development of spaces dominated by governmental systems and institutions, even though it does not extend to the individual, which is his main concern. He believes a reconsideration of Hegel to be especially timely because, rather than subscribing to the idea of a breakdown of the nation-state in favour of autonomous cities that become powerful because they are centers of information, as described by Saskia Sassen, Lefebvre believes that a state-like mentality is consolidating globally. This mentality is intent on reorganizing societies on a national basis using technology and information to do so, irrespective of political ideology. Sassen conceptualizes world city-states that evolve as concentrated antennae in a global transmission network. Robert Kaplan, a fellow at the New

Cesar Pelli: Petronas Towers (1996), Kuala Lumpur
The resolution of complicated geometries – facilitated by computers
– has resulted in a resurgence of traditional reinterpretations.

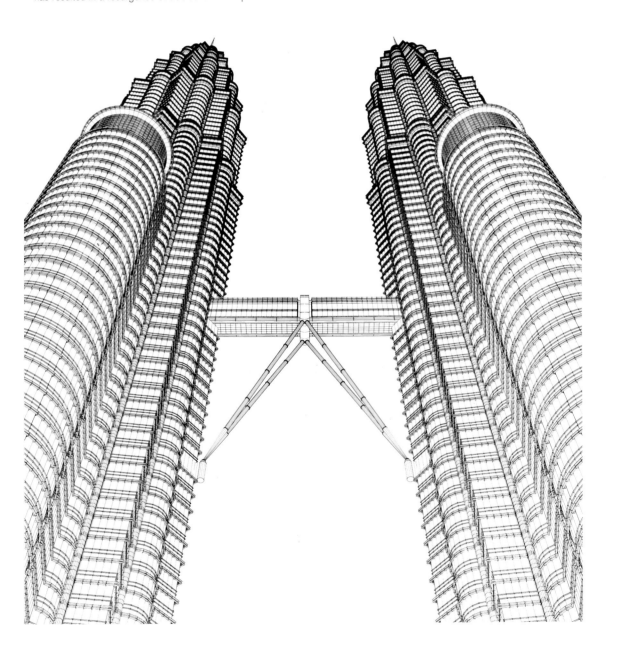

Nicholas Grimshaw & Partners: Eden Project (2000), Cornwall
The degradation of the environment has led to several attempts to create an
artificial substitute.

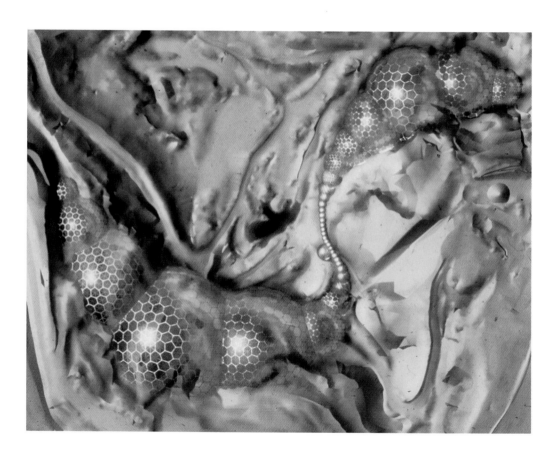

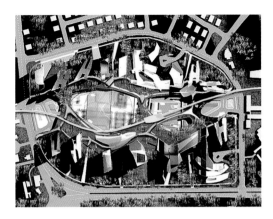

Hamzah and Yeang: BATC Tower, Setapak
The freedom allowed by the computer has inspired the breaking of conventions.

American Foundation, predicts that vast metroplexes will be the main political organizations of the future, amounting to vectors of prosperity that will pass through zones of instability all around the world. The subtle difference between these two concepts and the consolidated world state that Lefebvre describes is one of degree of control, the means used to achieve it, and the potential for revolt against it. [35] This vision of the future is one of incessant violence, an updated version of class struggle that makes the Earth First sit-ins by the disciples of George Mombio or the demonstrations in Seattle during the World Trade Organization conference in 1999 seem tame by comparison, and takes as a more likely model the persistent vicious war in Chechnia, but with more sophisticated technology.

The Four Implications of Social Space
Lefebvre maintains that his contention that social space exists and can be objectively studied has four important implications. The first of these is that as this global process of commodification intensifies, natural space will continue to disappear, as nature is increasingly considered as nothing more than a resource base to support it. Natural space will be "lost to view" and nature itself will be "lost to thought" as the powerful myths surrounding it diminish in meaning, and the utopia that it has historically represented is usurped by technological substitutes. The second implication is that each society has and still does produce its own space, with the spaces of reproduction – or of

"bio-physiological relations" between sexes and age groups – and those of production – or the hierarchical organization of labor – differing greatly before and after industrialization, after which the "social relations of production" add a third layer of complexity. But, in keeping with the awareness of the method of control identified by Edward Said as Orientalism in the late 1970s and extended by others, such as Homi Bhabha, into the question of the impossibility of cultural authenticity in the face of global homogenization, Lefebvre raises the important question of the difference between Western and non-Western space, the difficulty of transplanting concepts rooted in one culture into another, and of mutual understanding. This difficulty emerges, for example, in the perpetually recycled discussion about "Asian space" and how it differs from its Western counterpart, typically focusing on the lack of a tradition of public space in Asia compared to the plazas and piazzas of Europe, without sufficient recognition of the changes that exposure to, and emulation of, Western culture has wrought. The third implication provides the opportunity to further refine this post-industrial triad of reproduction, production, and the social relations of production, into the kinds of spatial experience that such social relations create. These spatial experiences divide into three categories. Spatial practice refers to the "sets" characteristic of each social configuration and interaction. The second category, perceived representations of space, refers to space as "encrypted reality" or as the conceptualized

NBBJ: Kwan Tong Town Center, Hong Kong
The future world now being realized via computer design
often seems alien to people.

impressions of scientists, architects, urban planners, and "social engineers." The third category is that of conceived and representational spaces, or spaces as they are lived and described in associated symbols and images. This last category, of bodily, lived experience, has lately been a rapidly burgeoning field of specialization in its own right, led by Maurice Merleau-Ponty and his landmark *Phenomenology of Perception*, followed by the work of Drew Leder. These three categories are considered to be interconnected, active, and non-abstract.

The fourth and final implication of this "science of space" is that the stories told in the passages between one social construct or "mode of production" and another are as important as the phases themselves, because of the contradictions that they bring into high-relief and the lessons these offer. Considered in this way, historical form becomes a spatial code to assist in interpretation and understanding, divided between pre-industrial absolute space, which was intrinsically symbolic, and post-industrial abstract space. Lefebvre describes this as the critical time "that productive activity (labor) became no longer one with the process of reproduction which perpetuated social life, but in becoming independent of that process, labour fell prey to abstraction…"[36]

The contradictions that are revealed in such passages give space texture, which is so far decidedly absent in the virtual realm, which is impoverished and mute however technically flashy it may be in comparison to the rich panoply of considerations just described, which provide an effective methodology for historical interpretation, contemporary extrapolation, and future change. In Lefebvre's definition of representations of space as an extension of material determinism, virtual space fits only as one small category, a culmination of neo-capitalist abstract space that is a by-product of globalization and a reductive negation of humanity. Virtual space cannot yet accommodate a generative framework that accounts for people and their complex patterns, ethnic difference, variegated context, nature, and cosmology, and instead confuses the exponential possibilities of a limited number of binary choices for an agent of social change.[37]

Virtual Space as the Realization of an Objectifying Mentality

The abstract space that Lefebvre refers to is fulfilled in its digital equivalent in a critical way. Several extensive studies of the role that perspective has played in the visualization and fabrication of abstract space appeared in the1990s, including Hubert Damish's *The Origin of Perspective* (1994), James Elkin's *The Poetics of Perspective* in the same year, and Alberto Pérez-Gomez and Louise Pelletier's *Architectural Representation and the Perspective Hinge* (1997). Of these, the Pérez-Gomez-Pelletier history addresses this technological realization of abstract space most directly. The final section of this exhaustive investigation into the reasons behind the transition from naturally occurring perspective to its artificial reconstruction from the Renaissance onward, entitled "Digital Space," is organized as an indictment of the "tyranny" that the authors identify as a potential danger in digital design. Their argument makes all that precedes it finally appear to be a polemical prelude to the important conclusion that the application of computers to architecture involves more than a new sophisticated tool that can be manipulated like a pencil or pen. It is, rather, "the culmination of the objectifying mentality of modernity and it is, therefore, inherently perspectival. Indeed, the invisible perspectival hinge operating in nineteenth-century axonometric space is internalized and made even more 'natural' by computer technology, resulting in a powerful tool of reduction and control. The tyranny of computer-aided design and its graphic systems can be awesome: because its rigorous mathematical base is unshakable, it rigidly establishes a homogeneous space and is inherently unable to combine different structures of reference." [38]

As evidence, Pérez-Gomez and Pelletier single out an image that appeared in an article entitled "Liquid Architecture" by Marcos Novak, who has since continued to grow in stature as one of the leading proselytizers for the idea that digital design is comparable to De Stijl constructions, formulated around three-dimensional, perspectival space. But, since that article appeared, in an anthology on cyberspace compiled by Michael Benedict in 1991 (cited here earlier), Novak's work has changed dramatically, more closely approximating the liquidity he praises. [39]

While the Pérez-Gomez-Pelletier conclusion shows that architectural representations in digital space are based in a modernist, perspectival mentality – and so by implication are part of the commodification inherent in that mentality – their work predates the fluidity of much of the avant-garde digital expression shown in this book, but they also predicted the important juncture that this liquidity represents. They warn that unless those using computers in architectural applications overcome the prevailing reliance on three-dimensional Cartesian spatial representations, they will never be able to achieve the full potential of this technology as an instrument of critical practice, in which ephemeral images, constructed in cyberspace, lead to hitherto unimaginable conceptual territory. This juncture between fluidity and reductive fixation is clearly demarcated today, with the majority of the programmes available to professionals and students falling into the latter category of "redundant self-referential formalism." What is also clearly evident is the challenge of translation back into buildable architecture once this fluidity is achieved, of converting ephemeral images into reality. Not too long ago, speculation about this conversion seemed to be entirely focused on Zaha Hadid, whose hand-drawn graphics have something of the quality of the most fluid digital representations, and the common constructivist denominator between them is a promising area of research yet to be addressed.

Jerde Partnership: Miramar Center, Taiwan
Because it exists in the interstitial, theoretical space between
Post-modernism and theming, which both thrived in urban
areas, entertainment architecture is most prevalent in the city.

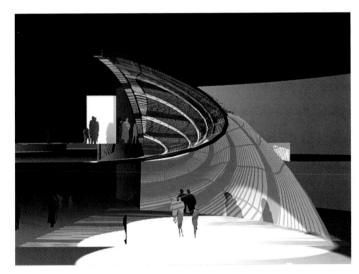 

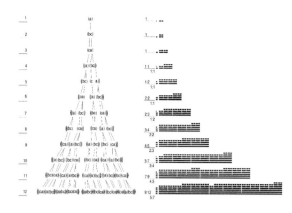

Karl Chu
The mathematical patterns that Chu is investigating also create elegant diagrams.

Context and Materiality

A second issue that arises, as a subset of this discussion of abstract space, is that of context, since in fulfilling the modernist method of objectification, virtual reality also represents the final realization of the myth that science can be value free, enacted through the rejection of direct experience and the attitude that reality is only valid if it can be statistically quantified. Digital space is quantified by a programmer, who enacts a simplification of reality through a process of abstraction in which empirical data that does not fit the chosen conceptual framework is discarded. [40]

This detachment, or disembodiment, coincides with a critical turning point in the history of human interaction with nature and the accelerating environmental degradation and resource depletion that has been the result, a point at which architects have an unprecedented opportunity to reassert leadership as ecological advocates and responsible stewards. It is also a point at which students especially should be made aware of the basic physical characteristics of the building materials available to them more thoroughly than is now typically the case, as well as of the global implications of the choices they make in terms of economic dependencies and rates of regeneration.

The Universal Construction as Exception

The programme developed by John Frazer at the Architectural Association in London is a laudable reaction to the danger of detachment from the natural context and to the reductive formalism that is inherent in digital design. Frazer has been involved in a search for a genetic algorithm that will allow the computer to emulate natural evolution by creating virtual architectural models that can respond to different environments. [41] This initiative began with the realization that existing computer-aided design programmes are geared toward the repetition of standard configurations, but are unable to produce new forms. If used thoughtlessly they have the tendency to dull the critical facilities which would normally allow a designer to realize that a concept is not well conceived much earlier in the process of development. Such programmes distort the design process to fit its integral limitations, forcing it to conform to an end product, and directing feedback to the most easily quantified aspects of the problem. [42] Frazer also believes that the current architectural design process is fundamentally flawed, and by emphasizing users' needs wants to use the computer to challenge current practice rather than to reinforce it. Rather than trying to reconfigure an existing CAD programme, Frazer decided to build a computer of his own and to programme it in a way that would replicate biological systems. The first of many was written at the Architectural Association between 1967 and 1968. This ultimately led to the building of the Universal Constructor in 1990 at the AA diploma unit 11. It did not use software, but was based on the establishment of first principles. The unit initially concentrated on working procedures, then learned and developed languages, developed machine codes and designed and built its own logic circuits, hierarchically building up single functions, just as they occur in nature. Frazer feels the real benefit of building the Universal Constructor was "in having to re-think explicitly and clearly the way in which we habitually do things… by externalizing and materializing the inner processes of the computer, our physical models act like any architectural model by assisting understanding and visualization." [43]

In the best tradition of A.M. Turing, who was one of the first to be interested in using the computer to model morphogenetic processes, the unit developed a genetic language that produced a "code script" of instructions that were then used to simulate the development of prototypical forms. These were then evaluated in various environments on the basis of conflicting criteria operating for selection and the way in which morphological and metabolic processes adapted to the interaction between a built form and each of these environments. "What we are evolving," Frazer explains, "are the rules for generating form rather than the forms themselves. We are describing processes, not components, ours is a packet-of-seeds as opposed to the bag-of-bricks approach." In this process, the architect becomes a "catalyser" rather than a designer, and the architecture "a form of artificial life, subject, like the natural world, to principles of morphogenesis, genetic coding, replication and selection." [44]

Karl Chu
The reproduction of evolutionary patterns in some of
Chu's designs is reinforced by natural colors.

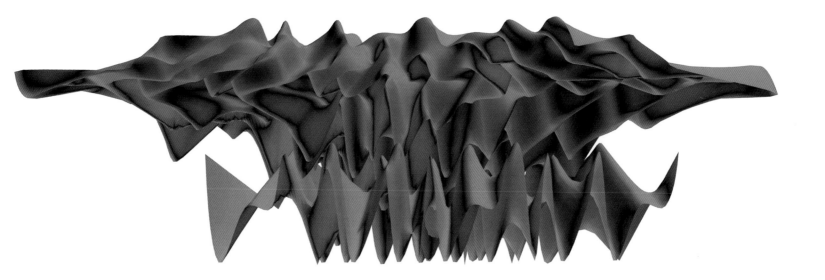

Karl Chu
By investigating the morphological similarities between building and concept, Karl Chu is revolutionizing the meaning of ecological architecture.

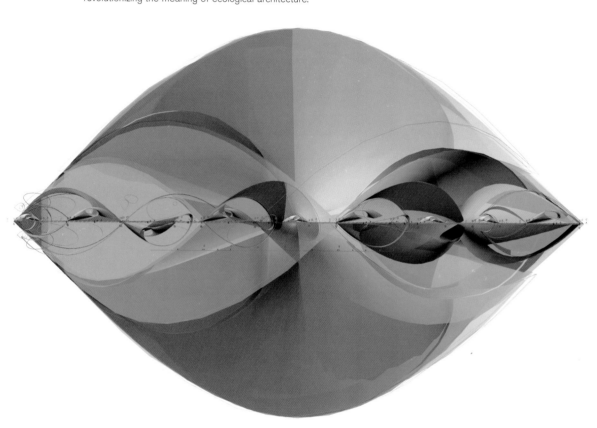

Hamzah and Yeang: BATC Tower, Setapak
The ecologically sustainable skyscraper seems like
an oxymoron, but computer simulations are helping
to make it a reality.

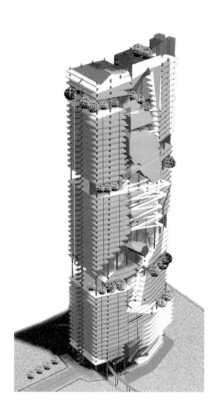

Exclusivity

Frazer's structured relegation of intention to the
computer raises a third issue, one concerning
the use of cyberspace as a sphere of control and
the existence of what has been referred to as the
digital divide, caused by the fact that no technology
is neutral, but has typically been used to enhance
power, authority, and privilege. There is a growing
awareness that the computer is central to a
pervasive form of technological imperialism,
consciously or subconsciously promoting Western
– principally American – values which translate into
spatial configurations in their CAD equivalent that
have yet to reflect the sophistication of Lefebvre's
cultural differentiation of space. For the foreseeable
future, digital resources will continue to be unequally
distributed, in spite of claims that the price of
telecommunications and computers continues to
fall so that everyone will eventually be able to
share in this technology. The issue is not the price
of an individual cell phone or PC, but bandwidth,
which will exacerbate the division between have
and have-not nations, and the class divisions
within them, at a critical point of development.

On the individual level, there is the worry of an
increase in antisocial tendencies, characterized by
Richard Sclove as the concern that "screen-based
technologies [are]… prone to induce democratically
unpromising psychopathologies, ranging from
escapism to passivity, obsession, confusing
watching with doing, withdrawal from other forms
of social engagement and psychological distancing
from moral consequences." [45]

In The 21st Century Project, intended to set
a new course for American policies related to
science and technology, a group called Computer
Professionals for Social Responsibility in Palo
Alto, California has identified the three critical
challenges of the coming century to be
environmental sustainability, global disarmament,
and equitable global development. They warn that
the continued control of critical technologies by
governmental-industrial partnerships, in what US
President Dwight Eisenhower once ominously
referred to as "the military-industrial complex,"
should be reviewed in a national open forum and
debate. Listing these critical technologies as
computer science, computer architecture,
networking, high-density data storage, digital
imaging, telecommunications, artificial intelligence,
robotics, micro and optics technologies, flexible
computer-integrated manufacturing, and high-
performance computing as well as materials
science and biotechnology research, they argue
that current structures perpetuate "elite
management" and a technology-driven policy
approach in the United States that has established
a "priesthood of experts in conflict with democratic
values." [46] Dissenters will undoubtedly point to
events such as the merger of Internet pioneer
America Online with Time Warner in January 2000
as overwhelming evidence of the democratization
of this technology, since it will lead to the worldwide digital distribution of interactive entertainment,
information, and consumer services that will be
accessible on a wide variety of receivers from

laptops to television sets – what the new conglomerate calls "an integrated consumer space." But others are alarmed at the trend that this merger portends, a trend toward the control of information by fewer and fewer sources, with alliances between other media giants such as Microsoft and Yahoo, or Disney and Viacom-CBS predicted for the future. The rule of the corporate jungle seems to be: merge or face the possibility of being crushed by the giant you have spurned. The driving motive behind the America Online-Time Warner merger, beneath a jointly stated desire to make a mass medium "part of the everyday habits of ordinary consumers," was the realization by the dominant online server that in the revolutionary transition from telephone cable to high capacity broadband fibreoptic networks, they would eventually become extinct unless they aligned with a company with access to this faster system. The broadband gateway that promises to widen the gap between rich and poor nations worldwide was decisive.

The 21st Century Project also raises the more complex issue of quality of life, of the degree to which public cultural development, education, health, and safety are a factor in governmental technological policy or are considered by America Online-Time Warner, Walt Disney, Viacom-CBS, News Corporation, Microsoft, AT&T, MCI Worldcom, Yahoo, Amazon.com or eBay as criteria for present or future mergers. The criteria of the "everyday habits of consumers," translates into potential for Internet sales with little concern for the well

documented deterioration of standards of educational competence in the United States, the alarming increase in violence in schools, the debasing of knowledge that has been the result of generalization on the Internet, the lack of a satisfactory health care system, the need for two wage earners in a family to maintain a minimal standard of living and the endemic "time-famine," to be discussed later, as an initial list. If one measure of democracy is the ability of people to individually influence social circumstances for the common good, a way for citizens to participate in determining social structure, then such technology cannot now be considered an empowering force in this process, although it does have the potential to be. The "virtual communities" that the Internet boasts discourage the kind of human interaction that fosters what Richard Sclove has identified as a "cornerstone of democracy," "as well as discouraging the practices that nurture collective efficacy, mutual respect, and moral and political equality, and that sustain commonality and physical and moral independence." [47]

Advocates of virtual community argue that people don't have to meet face to face to feel connected, and that the same criticisms now being leveled against the Internet could also be said to apply to the printing press and the telephone. They, however, were not typically based on anonymity and did not so completely filter out context. Since digital imaging in architecture is high up on the list of the critical technologies identified in The 21st Century Project,

professionals should consider how they can help, or lead, in recontextualizing computer-assisted design and in using it to improve the quality of life, rather than inadvertently exacerbating the social problems which are now being identified as being caused by it. Research conducted by the Stanford Institute for Quantitative Study of Society, for example, which is one of the first large-scale surveys of the social impact of the computer, took a random sample of 4,113 individuals over age 18. From their survey, they concluded that 55 percent of Americans have access to the Internet, and that time online means less time with friends and family, raising the prospect of more individual isolation and less social contact in the future. This brackets the warnings issued in *The Lonely Crowd*, written by David Riesman with Nathan Glazer and Reuel Denny at the onset of the mass media revolution in 1950, about the loss of community that it would cause. The progressive disintegration of social interaction that the Stanford study predicts also augments another survey carried out by researchers at Carnegie Mellon University, who identified higher levels of loneliness and depression among Internet users.

Hamzah and Yeang: Nagoya 2006 Tower
Intervention into a complex urban setting like Nagoya
has been made easier by the use of aerial studies.

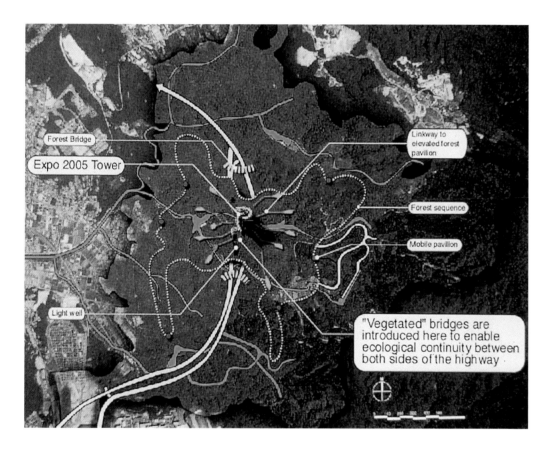

Environmental Simulation Center: Upper East Side Rezoning, New York City
The sytem used allows clients to "walk through" a proposed project.

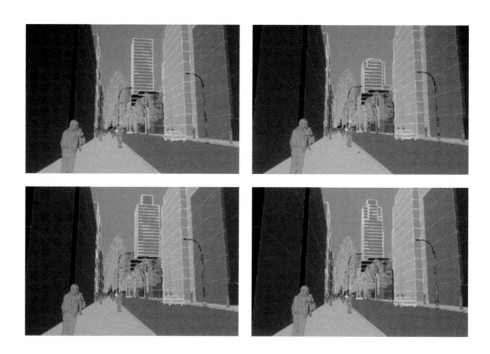

Giving People a Voice

Urban Simulation Laboratories are an inspiring contradiction to the claim that computers are inherently elitist. The first use of simulation technology in urban planning in the United States was at the University of California at Berkeley in the 1960s, and since then about ten laboratories have been established in North America, using a melange of techniques and programmes available for virtual reality, geographic information systems (GIS), computer-aided design, and flight simulation which have been adapted to various databases.

The Environmental Simulation Center, established in 1991 at the New School for Social Research in New York City, has been one of the most visible and arguably proactive of these. Now under the direction of Michael Kwartler, an architect and urban planner specializing in land use regulations, the Center has earned a reputation for impartiality and accuracy after having modeled projects in both urban and rural contexts over the last decade, making it especially effective as a lightning rod in conflict resolution during the participatory planning process that it implements. The majority of its work is in computer modeling, providing the mathematically accurate three-dimensional representations of a wide variety of data, as a way of quantitatively analyzing growth management plans, environmental impact, and zoning studies. In addition to GIS maps, which are usually a critical starting point, the necessary data is extrapolated from US Census Bureau statistics, aerial surveys, topographic surveys, insurance underwriters' documentation, and tax maps, combined to create high-definition, three-dimensional images at a wide variety of scales from streetscape to district. Due to the time involved in gathering, synthesizing, and converting this wide variety of information, computer simulation is expensive, but the Center typically seeks outside funding to make its services more affordable to a wide audience, since its main objective is to involve as many people as possible in the design process.

Urban, Edge City, Suburban, and Exurban Solutions

The Environmental Simulation Center initially focused on New York City, on the 14th Street rezoning study, and rezoning projects for Riverside South, the Upper East Side, the Grand Central Station Sub-District, the Lincoln Square Special Permit District, the Melrose Commons Urban Renewal Area, and a particularly energetic interactive community design workshop involving the neighborhood around the Frederick Douglass Circle in Upper Manhattan. The most publicized of its projects is a computer model of Lower Manhattan, part of its ongoing commitment to model the entire metropolitan area as a three-dimensional version of the geographic information system incorporating census, land use, building code, landmark, ownership, and other data, an ambitious undertaking made possible in part by Oracle relational database management software. In 1993 the model helped the New York City Planning Department revise zoning regulations for the high-density residential areas on the Upper East Side of Manhattan, its neutrality acting as a catalyst to help a number of agents – such as the Real Estate Board of New York, the American Institute of Architects, and a local civic association in addition to the Department of Planning – who would normally be antagonistic toward one another reach consensus. Their model of Second Avenue, from 78th to 87th Streets, was used to display the different zoning objectives of each of the participants in axonometric projection, helping all parties concerned to visualize the changes to the built environment that would result from their demands. By providing much more information on which to base a decision, the computer model became a way of clearly testing proposals, leading to consensus rather than contentious arguments about whose information was correct. This exercise was carried out with the memory of the film *Times Square* – commissioned by the Municipal Art Society and produced by Peter Bosselman of UC Berkeley – still fresh in everyone's mind. *Times Square* had criticized what was characterized as the imminent over-development of the Theater District and was followed by another film, narrated by a well known Hollywood actor, called *No More Tall Stories*, which, by asking for the rezoning of Upper East Side Avenues, had antagonized many people and politicized the development issue. The independence of the Center was therefore crucial, since everyone realized that the views and angles used to visualize each proposal could be manipulated to promote

**Environmental Simulation Center:
Princeton Junction project**
There has been a quiet revolution going on in urban mapping, which is slowly becoming legible in the transformation of entire communities.

some at the expense of others if the proposals were not carried out by an objective body.

One clear example of the versatility and usefulness of computer simulation in the Manhattan studies is the Center's analysis of ways to develop regulatory approaches to revitalize Lower Manhattan, involving the Financial District, the area around the World Trade Center and Battery Park City, since earlier projects had not succeeded in changing the lifeless character of this area after offices close. The Environmental Simulation Center identified the key parameter of pinpointing buildings 180 feet (55 meters) high above sea level, or of more typically about 15 stories above the street, with 8,000 square feet (740 square meters) of space or less, reasoning that if existing office buildings could be converted to residential and commercial use, it would attract residents who would keep the streets alive after five, and that they would prefer having apartments or condominiums with a view. By clearly identifying the candidates for residential conversion, the Center demonstrated the viability of the proposal to the law-makers who were deciding the fate of legislation on it.

Some of the many projects outside New York City that have involved interactive community planning and design are the Princeton Junction Case Study completed in August 1994, the New York-New Jersey Highlands Demonstration Planning Project involving the City of Newark and the township of West Milford, of September 1996, the Melrose neighborhood study in the Bronx,

better known as the "Nos Quedamos" project, in January 1997, and the Ascutney Vermont study in December 1999. These projects are important because of the comparative issues they raise. Princeton Junction was the classic "Edge City," without political boundaries, a rapid-growth area along the Route 1 Corridor in West Windsor, New Jersey. Full of office parks, retail malls, townhouse condominium developments, and single family suburban subdivisions that had sprung up after World War II, it had a busy commercial strip but no center. Michael Kwartler set out to determine if Princeton Junction was the proper place for a center for West Windsor, and if a typical edge city should have one at all. Superficially, the junction seemed suitable as a center, since it was a crossroads close to the north-south transportation spine of Route 1, East-West Highways Route 571 and Alexander Road, and the Princeton Junction Railroad Station, handling thousands of commuters each day. The project offered a litany of problems associated with the edge city condition that, if solved, promised to make it a prototype; such as how to adapt a parade of convenience stores, gas stations, and professional offices originally designed for easy automobile access to pedestrian use and then connect them to transit in a functionally and aesthetically pleasing way. Added to this were the difficulties of tying the single-family neighborhood to the south, which is a major source of pedestrian traffic to the station, and a commuter parking lot to the west into a cohesive system, and of making a rather mundane station

an attractive focal point. Planning consultants Lenaz, Muellar and Associates had developed a plan that already proposed a Town Square that would link land use with transit, encourage mixed use and create a pedestrianized town center, but the plan gave little indication of what this center would actually look like. The Environmental Simulation Center provided a "Suburban Centers Kit of Parts" derived from both generic suburban conditions and the specific elements of this particular situation to allow West Windsor township's residents to interactively make their existing masterplan a three-dimensional reality. The core area was mapped using AES computer graphics software; an aerial photograph was scanned, digitized, and then adjusted to fit the Geographical Information System maps to create a new two-dimensional computer map that provided finer-scale information about building locations than that found on the 1:24,000 scale United States Geographical Survey quadrant maps. This map was then further refined using tax and engineering maps, and once building heights could be established with additional aerial and ground-level photography, a three-dimensional base map was created. Then a series of meetings was scheduled with planning board members and other planners, architects, landscape architects, developers, and land use attorneys to determine how the "Kit of Parts" could best be used to establish design guidelines that would contextualize Princeton Junction as well as similar "edge cities" throughout the state. They found that

Environmental Simulation Center: West Milford, Connecticut
The notion that social and cultural differences can be accommodated by superficial substitution is debatable, but such differences are represented in the "Kit of Parts" system developed by the Simulation Center.

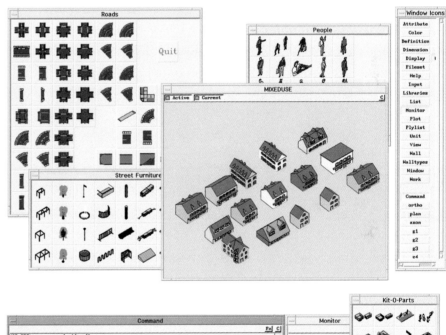

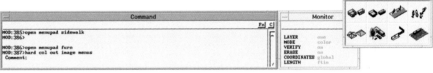

the solution was to first create a document that showed the approximate retail, residential, and institutional square footages, which could then be matched up with the standardized modules in the Kit to provide a general framework that town residents could then work on, rather than determining a specific close-end design proposal.

An Adaptable Kit of Parts

Not surprisingly, many of the architects involved in this first series of meetings criticized the Kit as not being specific enough, but eventually all participants reached consensus on a list of strategies that would improve the fragmentation of the built environment. These include unifying landscape; standardized lot sizes; building heights and set-backs; similar building materials; a "main street" with controlled signage, shop windows, and entrances; more clearly established landmarks; gateways and architecture that promoted a civic identity; more public space, including a town square, using bordering elements like arcades, colonnades, and terraces; and more attention paid to linkages such as streets, primary and secondary pedestrian promenades, and pathways. If these sound familiar, then similarity to New Urbanist manifestos will be discussed later.

The "Kit of Parts" approach proved to be a resounding success on its first outing at Princeton Junction, effectively demonstrating how much the character of the proposed town center could be changed by implementing various building heights and set-backs. Rather than being excluded, the

Environmental Simulation Center:
Ascutney, Vermont, town planning project
The repercussions of various legislative scenarios can now be tested
beforehand, using programs like Policy Simulator for town planning.

Environmental Simulation Center:
Melrose Commons, New York
Sequential spatial readings and animation help users and
clients more easily visualize new plans.

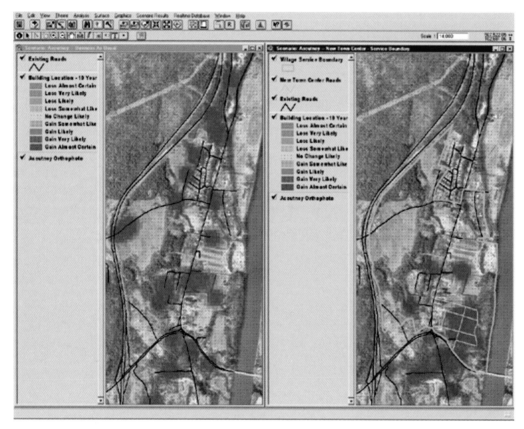

design professionals involved in the exercise also found that they were instrumental in setting up the parameters of each proposed solution and evaluating each alternative. Everyone concerned was surprised at the extent to which chores that had previously proven to be very tedious, such as relating building size to parking and zoning requirements, were calculated instantaneously; concluding that this was one essential strength of the simulation technique. The more quantified information that was provided, such as parking requirements, tax ratables, traffic variations, and environmental constraints, the better the results, making all the laborious effort put into creating a digitized map of the entire township at the outset worthwhile.

Town Centers Are Over

The most important discovery at Princeton Junction, with critical implications for similar "edge cities" elsewhere, was that finally, the concept of a single town center was just not feasible, given existing zoning codes, and that multiple retail centers were an inevitable part of such peripheral developments. The "Kit of Parts", which was programmed around the preconceived notion of a single town center, was too successful in demonstrating to local residents the difference between what was proposed and the pattern of suburban sprawl that already existed; the changes necessary were obviously more structural and societal than dropping a new traditional core into this atomized utopia. [48]

At West Milford, New Jersey two years later, the "Kit of Parts" was closely modeled on the architectural, urban design, and ecological characteristics of the area; an advisory committee participated in its design. The problem in this instance was that in the late 1980s, West Milford and the City of Newark were locked in a lawsuit over the zoning of 18,000 acres (7,300 hectares) which affected the township's ability to raise taxes – in effect making this a classic case of suburban growing pains in the attempt to impose substantially higher ratables on what was primarily a rural area. Once again, the Environmental Research Center provided a neutral sounding board for a diverse cast of characters in a controversial situation, trying to work out a reasonable agenda for future growth in the township; to arrive at a viable series of alternative development solutions that would be compatible with local community character, conform with state and local planning and fiscal objectives, and provide a reasonable return on investment for local property owners and developers.

The same process of compiling background information, such as GIS and tax maps, was used to create a three-dimensional computer model; the difference between this exercise and Princeton Junction was that this was "exurbia," the area of fastest growth in the United States as the suburbs become saturated and modems allow a new contingent of subcontracted employees to work from offices at home without commuting. Once again the issues raised promised to be prototypical,

and these emerged as the need to preserve the character of the existing landscape and town, and to maintain a sound economic base for the community, making the future of a forest surrounding the town, the amount of open space designated for recreation, the kind of future retail, and the level of population density the central focus of the exercise.

This was also the case in the smaller town of Ascutney, Vermont, in which the Center is still involved, where the same issues of compact versus dispersed growth are now being debated. Developing the village center in this small town of 800 people will require a large financial investment in new infrastructure, while outlying development would substantially alter the character of the community and affect ground water quality. In this case Michael Kwartler used a software called Community Works, based on Arc View (a geographic information system) as well as Multi Gen Paradigm's military flight simulation software, Price Waterhouse Cooper's forecasting models, and Foresite Consulting's scenario and impact analysis tools. Community Works has three components, a "Townbuilder" module that enables users to visualize alternative development scenarios, a second "Scenario Constructor/Impact Analysis" module component for testing policy parameters such as density, trip generation, and infrastructure costs, and a third "Policy Simulator" module that predicts the land use, demographic, and economic changes that would result from various policies. In a typical block, for example, using local lot dimensions and house types, various floor-area ratios, lot coverage dimensions, setbacks, and height restrictions can be proposed to see how they affect development patterns, visual character, and traffic. The difference between Community Works and Photoshop, 3D Analyst, or CAD is the detail of the modeling on the buildings, and the ability for the viewer to "walk" down the street. The software uses an IBM compatible platform, with a minimum 30 MHz processor, 12.8 megabytes of RAM, a Windows NT operating system, and a graphics card, making it easily accessible for citizen use in public hearing rooms.

One key to the system is the sensitivity used in altering the "Kit of Parts" to conform to local conditions, since this is a selective, subjective process. In the South Bronx neighborhood of Melrose, primarily made up of working class residents of Caribbean origin, the vernacular architecture of that region was evoked in many small details, such as a diagonal pattern of crosshatching on the trellises and railings to recall the small wooden cottages or *casitas* found around community gardens in rural Puerto Rico. The South Bronx project was one of the most proactive that the Environmental Simulation Center has been involved in because the neighborhood, of more than 5,000 residents, was scheduled for clearance in the New York City Urban Renewal Plan in late 1995. Residents appealed to the Bronx Center Committee and persuaded the city to allow them nine months to propose an alternative plan, which they, rather than professional planners working for

the city, were to produce. Instead, city and borough planning officials came to Melrose to meet with the neighborhood group, called "Nos Quedamos" or "We are Staying," to collaborate on the new plan, which Magnusson Architecture and Planning, a local firm familiar with the case, and Michael Kwartler, helped to facilitate. A protracted "battle of images" followed, which took place while Nos Quedamos carried out an extensive house by house survey of the neighborhood. This information, which the city did not have, put the local organization in a stronger position during the negotiations that followed, eventually resulting in a "town center" clustered around a listed courthouse, "main street" zoning along Melrose Avenue, more commercial activity along other major streets, and an evenly distributed network of landscaped open spaces.

Digital Technology Now Reaping What It Has Sown

There is considerable irony in the fact that simulation strategies such as this are primarily being used to evaluate the detritus of the information age, raising what Michael Kwartler has identified as three main issues. The first, he explains, "concerns the profound changes the city is undergoing as it has moved from a predominantly manufacturing economy to a service economy. Spurred on by the digital revolution and the changing nature and decentralization of work, the city's neighborhoods, districts, residences, and apartments are becoming increasingly mixed-use, notwithstanding the Zoning Resolution's fixation

with single purpose districts and unenforceable and arbitrary regulations regarding working at home and home occupations."[49] Second are the implications of substituting such single-purpose districts with mixed-use communities of the kind examined in the case studies just discussed, and the third is what Kwartler describes as "process values and the city's desire to minimize the impact of regulation on market decision making and individual initiative."[50]

The computer simulation technique is catching on; the National Capital Planning Commission now requires all architects working on projects on public land in Washington, DC, to submit three-dimensional computer models, which are then tested against a citywide model and incorporated into it if built. Using such a model of the proposed World War II memorial, the planners were particularly interested to see if the project blocked views of the Lincoln Memorial and other historical monuments on the Washington Mall using pedestrian-level perspectives that are typically or intentionally inaccurate in more conventional graphic presentations. For the generic architect's office, the tools for urban simulation range from a high-range Unix station to a Pentium class PC with a graphics card, with software that can get pricey, including Viz by Autodesk, Micro Station by Bentley Systems and Creator by Multi Gen Paradigm for three-dimensional construction and Vega and Game Gen by Multi Gen Paradigm for real-time simulation.[51]

While this provides what Kwartler has called a level of "accountability," the simulations are still

Moore, Ruble, Yudell: Miramar Villas, Guzelce, Turkey
The difficulties in laying out a completely new neighborhood have
been alleviated by computer simulation.

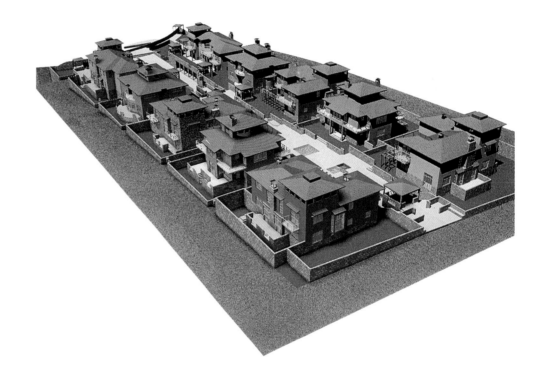

subjective interpretations of reality rather than an
accurate depiction of it, also subject to another
level of manipulation in the choices of views that
are shown, and as yet unable to approximate
the filter of grit that is part of the real urban
experience. But for a general public that finds it
difficult to understand conventional plans, sections,
and elevations and for whom cardboard models
are also too abstract, computer simulation is a
promising development that may finally make
participatory community design at the scale once
envisioned by Charles Moore in the 1980s, and
partially implemented by him, finally possible.
He may be faulted for trying to guide the entire
procedure in a preconceived direction, since the
final results of such community workshops always
ended up looking like his own, but he was one of
the first and the few to even consider giving up
control of the design process in this way. In an
unsung article entitled "You Have to Pay for the
Public Life," which is largely forgotten because it
appeared at the same time as Robert Venturi's
Complexity and Contradiction in Architecture in
the mid-1960s, Moore blamed the media for the
destruction of the public realm in contemporary
life, and in examining Southern California found
the freeways and Disneyland to be the only
obvious pathetic substitutes. The technology he
decried may now finally allow the return of the
responsibility for the creation of the public realm
to the people, and give architects the opportunity
to be facilitator in the process. [52]

Karl Chu
The transition from three-dimensional simulation to buildable
form is obviously the next challenge in Chu's process.

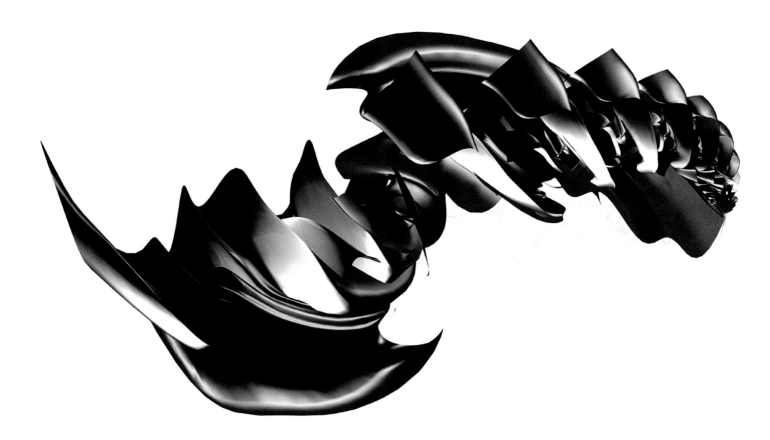

Computer Simulation and the New Urbanism

It is no coincidence that there is a great deal of similarity between the objectives articulated by Michael Kwartler on the impact of zoning on urban form and those voiced in the New Urbanist manifesto. Although not stated as clearly in the first idealistic polemic to appear since the numerous manifestos issued by Modernist and Futurist factions prior to World War II, the New Urbanist Charter concentrates on attacking the causes of urban isolation, suburban edgeness, and exurban exploitation at their legal source, rather than by proposing only the formal solutions that have identified them. By concentrating on changing zoning laws that favor outdated, industrial segmentation and which do not reflect the social changes that have resulted from the digital revolution, the New Urbanists have become the unlikely allies of computer simulation laboratories worldwide. Their common ground is one important zone of potential activism for architects in the future, regardless of ideological affiliation, if they want to avoid the onus of exclusivity.

Spirituality

Techno-visionary Arthur C. Clarke, who collaborated with Stanley Kubrick as an advisor on the supercomputer HAL in *2001: A Space Odyssey*, sees cybernetics as the fulfillment of technological determinism, believing that "it may be our role on the planet is not to worship, but to create God, and then our work will be done." Rather than computers being the tool that we use to create the built environment, in this scenario we become their tools, or more accurately, we become one with them. As a prelude to this fulfillment, the vacuum created by the precipitous decline of religious faith in the West at the end of the twentieth century is being filled with an unquestioning belief in digital technology at the beginning of the twenty-first, and this new religion, like the one it has supplanted, has an intricate set of power mechanisms all its own.[53] This idea of cyber-technology as a substitute religion, viewed historically, is the culmination of the systematic dismantling of the spirituality associated with organized religion by reason and the scientific method during the Enlightenment. Variously referred to as "technophilia," "technopaganism", or "technosis", this new religion, as described by Mark Dery, "has become an ironic repository of teleological visions and transcendentalist myths," a curious mixture of Sixties psychedelia and Nineties cyberdelia in which "God is progress, utopia is heaven and hell is deprivation: the lack of instant gratification."[54] And in it, as in the conventional organized religions it has supplanted, faith offers a way to deny the inherent weaknesses of the human condition and the inevitability of death.[55]

The post-modern acknowledgement of difference and the interest in Eastern religions that this has fostered in the post-industrial West now dovetails nicely with the disembodiment of cyberspace, a new post-corporal, sacred zone which Nicole Stenger has identified as similar to Mircea Eliade's concept of hierophany. This is "an irruption of the sacred that results in detaching a

Karl Chu
The organic unfolding of form connects Chu's architecture to nature.

territory from the surrounding corresponding milieu and making it qualitatively different." [56] Both share discontinuity, a "gap in the plane of reality", that makes each a sacred precinct. Where this disembodiment differs from eastern religious traditions, such as Buddhism, Taoism, Hinduism, and Sufism, is that each of these does not completely negate physical experience and each in varying degrees acknowledges a connection between the act of making and morality, which was also central to the Arts and Crafts argument. Sufism in particular concentrates on the idea of achieving moral growth through manual labor – the more repetitive the more uplifting – the point being self-realization rather than escapism. The connection between moral development and the physical process of making remains elusive, but concerns are surfacing that computers tend to encourage obsessive-compulsive behavior in some, shifting the focus to cognitive development instead of physical involvement and the emotional, moral, and spiritual growth it can bring, exacerbating a split between reason and emotion. [57]

Concern about this split has obvious implications for architects since it directly affects the nature of the creative act and the time involved in conception. The cumulative quality of design with the traditional tools of pencil, crayon, or pen and the materiality of graphically etching paper arguably enhanced meaning and purpose because it was an iterative process that allowed intuitive adaptation and time for the concept to grow.

Speed does not preclude meaning since creative purpose is adapted to, or adapts conditions to its use. But it remains to be seen if the quality of timelessness, which has historically been a common denominator in all great architecture, can be achieved once cumulative iteration is replaced by an instantaneous alternative. This quality of timelessness is consistently the result of an evolution of meaning and values rather than momentary fragmented, individual inspiration, but it may be that change has so completely replaced permanence at the core of the contemporary ethos, because the commercialization of architecture, as just another commodity, is now so complete, and spiritual emptiness is so endemic, that timelessness no longer has any value. [58]

Coop Himmelb(l)au: Expo 2001, Biel, Switzerland
If possible, the increased potential provided by the
computer has made the spatial theory of Coop
Himmelb(l)au even more extreme.

Coop Himmelb(l)au: Expo 2001
Monumental towers change the perception of scale in a
public space.

Liberation

The utopian dream of rational disembodiment – of complete liberation from physical limitations through a metamorphosis with machines – is nothing new, but is now much closer to becoming a reality. Popularized by Manfred Clynes in 1960, when he combined the words cybernetic and organism, the term cyborg was introduced at a time when medical advances in transplant surgery made the human body seem to be just a source of spare parts that are now "harvested" by hospitals much more systematically over the Internet. [59] Now, following on Arthur C. Clarke's contention that it is the destiny of the next generation not to seek, but to create God, Ray Kurtzweil has begun to speculate, in detail, how this prediction is being fulfilled. In *The Age of the Spiritual Machine: When Computers Exceed Human Intelligence* Kurtzweil transfers the idea of a hybrid cyborg from the realm of science fiction into reality, describing how the interchange of computer circuitry and the human brain will allow us to redesign ourselves with biological evolution replaced by a far less random technological equivalent. [60] The dramatic reduction in the size of circuits will soon allow them to be implanted in the neurons of the brain, allowing memory to be "unsubstantiated," or downloaded to an external database, or to be supplemented with digital memory and the Internet. Kurtzweil cites the successful implantation of silicon chips in human brains now, in operations to combat Parkinson's disease, and predicts that as biotechnology continues to reduce their size, microscopic, self-replicating, robotic chips, or nanobots, will be able to be injected into the blood stream and targeted to interact with every capillary and neuron in the brain, communicating with each other in what would essentially be a wireless network. The technology that has made this possible is the discovery at Rice University, Houston, of the nanotube, a carbon molecule hundreds of times stronger than steel, which has a greater computing capacity than silicon, making it possible to programme a synthetic device the size of a blood cell and through neural stimulation to finally implant virtual reality. [61]

Molecular Electronics

Nanotechnology and computer modeling have helped genome engineers to determine the exact DNA sequences of 24 different organisms, the codes of life that will allow new organisms to be created. The Human Genome Project, sponsored by the United States Government, is based on reconstructing the biochemical pathways of microorganisms, designing the genome structure of these microbes so that they will be able to perform biochemical functions, including molecular electronics. These microbes will be instructed to fabricate the complex electronic circuits of the wireless network Kurtzweil describes. [62] Computer modeling has also allowed researchers to identify gene pathways that have survived the test of evolution and to use a process called "DNA Shuffling" to generate new enzymes and organisms using natural selection. These organisms will be much more efficient because mutations have been deliberately introduced to strengthen them.

Kurtzweil estimates that it will be 30 years before the hybrid brain he predicts becomes a reality. In the meantime, technical liberation has taken on a more pragmatic urgency. At the dawn of the information age, only two decades ago, electronic technology was heralded as a means of salvation from boring repetitive jobs, eliminating long commutes by allowing people to work at home, increasing leisure time, providing more opportunities for personal development and creativity, eliminating environmental destruction and class stratification by replacing industrial wealth with knowledge as a source of national capital. [63]

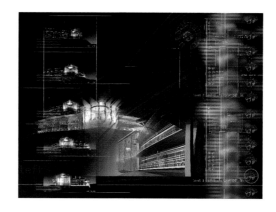

Softmirage: Think Tank
This multi-media visual presentation company uses
SOFTIMAGE, the software developed for creating the
special effects in such movies as *Jurassic Park*.

Time Famine

What has happened instead, in the shift from a
manufacturing to a service economy, is that
predictable working hours measured by punching
a time clock have been replaced by corporate
emphasis on projects with fixed deadlines, to
produce a new website, for example, and workers
put in many unclaimed overtime hours because
they are in a competitive, high-pressure
environment. The unprecedented economic
expansion in the United States has undoubtedly
been fueled by new electronic technologies.
The result is that people make more money, but
enjoy it less, because they are overworked and
have no time to enjoy life.[64] The unofficial pressure
to work longer hours and not claim overtime has
raised the national productivity rate but the
personal cost has been high. The Bureau of Labor
Statistics reports that 19 percent of Americans
now work more than 49 hours a week, up from
16 percent in 1985, and The Economic Policy
Institute estimates that together, parents in middle
class families work an average of 3,335 hours
per year, compared to 3,200 a decade ago, and
3,000 hours a year in 1979, or an increase of
eight weeks of work a year in the last 20 years.
Internationally, hours worked per person per year
now rank as: United States 1,966, Japan 1,889,
Canada 1,732, Britain 1,731, and Norway 1,399.

But these statistics, as indicative as they are of
an overworked global technocracy, do not tell the
whole story.[65] The web, laptop, modem, e-mail, cell
phone, and pager culture that is the reality of the
electronic revolution has blurred the boundaries
between work and leisure to the extent that work
never stops. The amount of information available
and the rapid changes in the technology that
delivers it have also made that work much more
complex, causing a "productivity paradox," or
disparity between time spent on knowledge-based
work and the value generated per unit of time
spent. Rather than liberating us, the information
we believe we control now controls us.

The implications for architects, aside from
the additional hours now added to an already
time-intensive profession, involve accommodating
entirely new kinds of spaces, since many
employees practically live in virtual environments.
The digital enclave that Eric Moss has been
designing over the last two decades, for example,
discussed in detail in Chapter IV, predicts that
these new offices must be far more flexible and
egalitarian than even the most radical open
landscape arrangements of conventional corporate
experience. His unprecedented Culver City
experiment is based on the notion of a world
within; communal spaces that provide a respite
from long hours spent in front of a screen, since
more and more time is now spent with co-workers
than with family, also requiring larger-scale visual
distractions that provide dimensional relief in an
interior environment intentionally deprived of
natural light.

Eric Owen Moss: Culver City (1987–), Los Angeles
The complex interaction of contiguous buildings on the site –
made possible by acquiring the air rights over an abandoned
railroad track – has been facilitated by a computer.

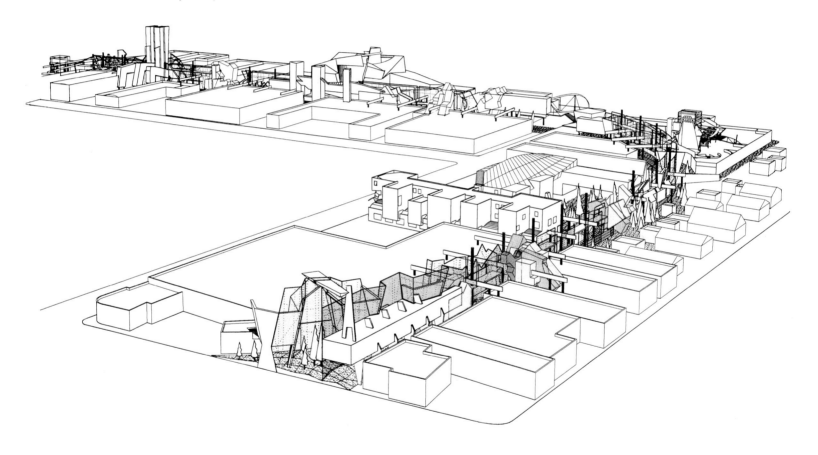

Softmirage: Lotus Bridge
Virtual experts (and the simulations they provide) have
now emerged as an intermediary between architects,
engineers, and clients.

Softmirage: Alpha Space
The selection of a background can dramatically change
the character of an image.

Coop Himmelb(l)au: Expo 2001 Biel, Switzerland
A dramatic *noir* background now seems very fashionable.

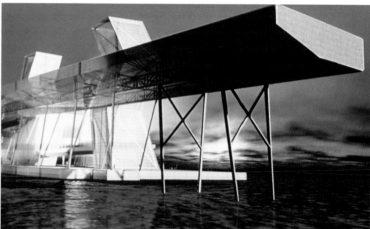

Karl Chu
Chu has an inner vision of a new world he feels
is still in an embryonic state.

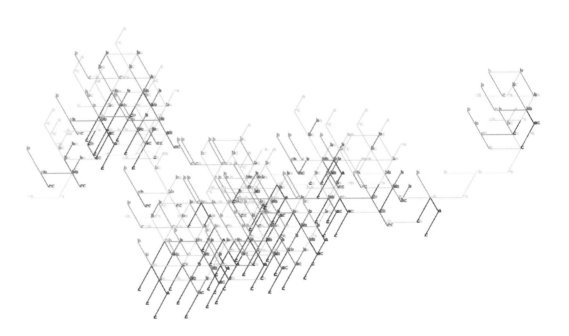

String Theory to the Rescue

The necessity for the "periodizing" that Jamison talks about has now extended to the obligatory attachment of theory to major new architectural movements. Post-modernism began with Jean-François Lyotard and Jean Baudrillard and continues to expand as the previous discussion about Lefebvre indicates. Deconstruction was partially initiated as a deliberate attempt by Peter Eisenman to literally interpret Jacques Derrida's search for the "in-between" at the Wexner Center and Aronoff Gallery, most prominently, and then Class Theory was commandeered as an explanation of orderly disorder. Sustainability owes much to Jurgen Habermas. And now, right on cue, String theory has appeared as the physical, mathematical equivalent of the most ephemeral and amorphous digital forms, offering sympathetic explorations of virtual space and time. In the same way that an actor works in bit parts for years before becoming an "overnight" sensation, String theory has been waiting in the wings for more than 25 years, supported by only a handful of physicists who realized that it alone had the potential of solving several intractible space-time mysteries. A breakthrough came in 1984 when a group including John Schwarz, now at Cal Tech in the United States, French physicists André Neven and Joel Scherk, and British physicist Michael Green were able to eliminate some theoretical inconsistencies, and firmly establish the number of dimensions involved at eleven; adding seven to Einstein's well tested theory of three dimensions of space and one of time. Most important of all, the eleventh dimension, which had proven to be the most troublesome outlier, was a graviton, a particle of gravity that provided an important bridge between the micro scale of quantum mechanics and macro scale of general relativity, allowing the seemingly irreconcilable aspects of particle theory and the theory of gravity to suddenly make sense. These seven extra dimensions imply that every particle in the universe, instead of being a point in space, is joined into strings in harmonic chords that form planes, with each string vibrating differently according to the particles it contains. By linking infinitesimally small particles to gravity, String theory offers the key to finally answering the mystery of the origin of the universe, since it began as a singularity governed by the laws of quantum mechanics, with gravity performing at small scale.

Karl Chu
Algorithms are only the beginning of Karl Chu's investigations.

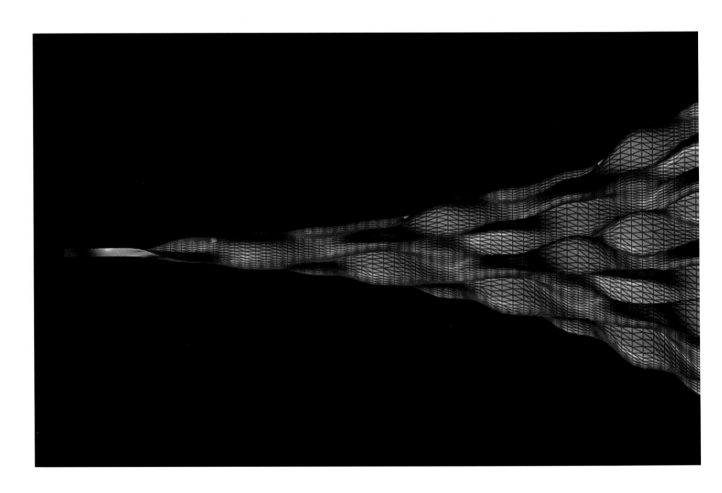

Membrane or Matrix Theory

In 1995 Edward Witten, of the Institute for Advanced Study at Princeton, precipitated another advance in String theory by introducing the idea that the planes of strings are actually vibrating membranes, allowing reconciliation of five variations of String theory that had evolved by then and holding out the promise that it may eventually lead to the universal mathematical equation Einstein was searching for. The concept that our universe may be one thin membrane among many literally gives new dimension to the old question of where it ends. String theory solves the disparity between the relative weakness of gravity and strength of electrical, magnetic, and nuclear forces since gravity can "leak out" of the membrane and the latter forces can't, and promises to make current space-time theory and causality irrelevant. [66]

Several Scenarios

All of these issues appear in varying degrees in the work presented here, as architects come to grips with their profound implications in various individual ways. The first and most uncomplicated of these is to use this powerful new digital potential as a tool to enhance design carried out in the same traditional way, usually identified with architects who had already established a signature "style" before the electronic tidal wave hit. They typically use AutoCAD for mechanistic, repetitive tasks, for hardlining graphically defined concepts. Chapter I reviews several of the most high-profile examples to help shed some light on this approach. Chapter

II discusses how this direction has been dramatically refined in a specialized CATIA application developed by Frank Gehry, which has received the most media and public attention through the Guggenheim Museum in Bilbao, Spain. This represents a singular conformation of technology to personal creative sensibilities.

Gehry's significant breakthrough is followed in Chapter III by a review of the alternative to using the computer as a subordinate alter ego, which is for the designer to let it lead; to follow digital cues in a back and forth dance. While certainly not exhaustive, the projects presented bracket the most recognizable variations of this approach, causing a great deal of excitement and proselytizing zeal today. Chapter IV discusses a third variant: not using the computer as a tool or a muse, but that of stopping the design process at critical breakpoints to interject hand drawn, graphic solutions, which are either scanned in or introduced in other ways, sometimes with an attitude of technological counterinsurgency. Finally, the way that computers are being used in architectural schools today is a key concern, affecting the future of the profession; the focus here, in Chapter V, is on a typical example, reflecting the mainstream in the United States at least, and selected for review because of personal experience.

Yuwen Peng: Sunset house
The diagrammatic approach, as used for this house design, seems
to appeal to some clients more than the three-dimensional one.

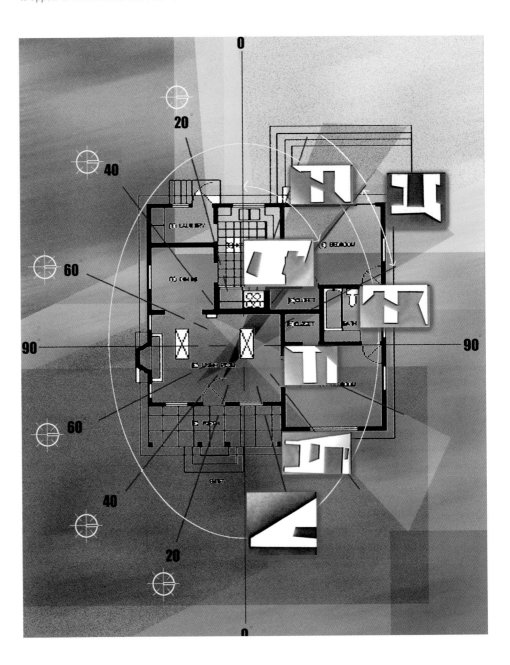

NOX: Off the Road
Even mundane forms, such as the ones in this project, look intriguing in digital renderings.

Moore, Ruble, Yudell: Sun Law Power Station competition (2000), Los Angeles
For many firms, adaption to the computer has required a change in their theoretical stance, creating a graphic/digital hybrid.

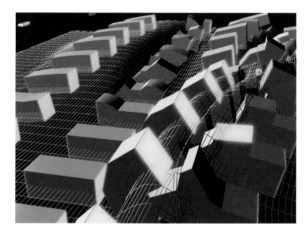

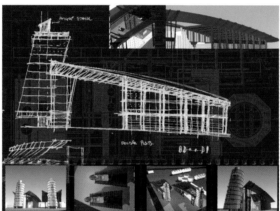

Frank Gehry: Guggenheim Museum (1997), Bilbao
The Bilbao Guggenheim represents an important breakthrough
in the use of the CATIA system in architecture.

**Behnisch, Behnisch and Partner: North German State
Clearing House Bank, Hannover**
Many architects continue to rely on traditional cardboard models
and combine them with computer modeling during design.

chapter 1
mechanical alter ego:
the computer as cybertool

70

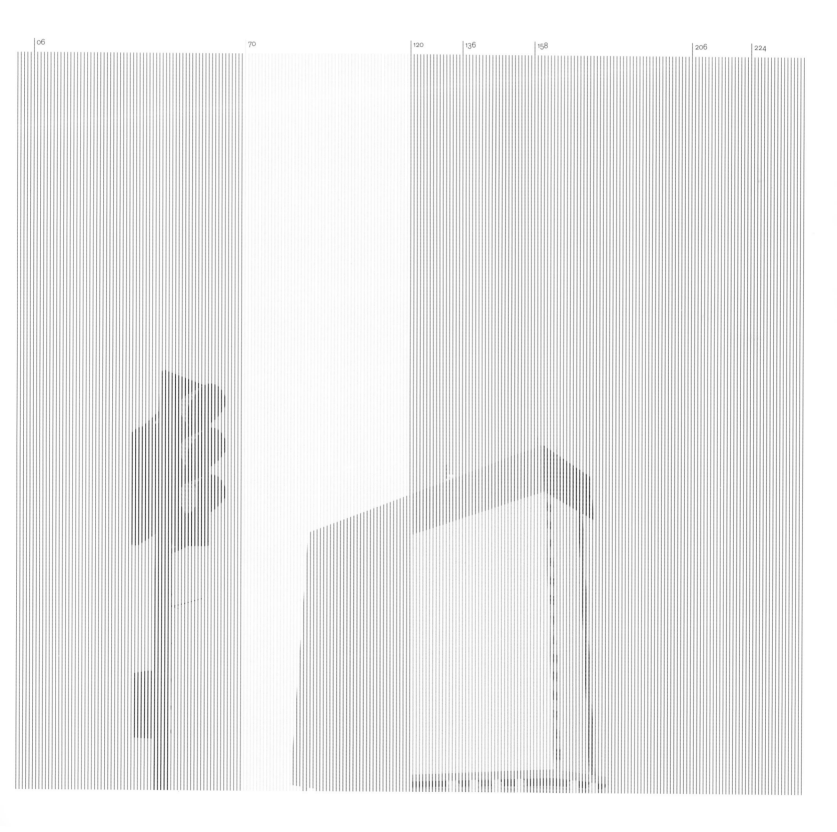

List of software:
Just a few of the many packages available to
architects are listed here.

Advanced Graphics Systems	VISIONAEL	Ditek International	DynaCADD (Windows)
Accugraph Corp.	Mountain Top	EDS GDS Solutions	GDS
Alias Research Inc	Alias Sonata	Engineered Software	PowerDraw
American Small Business Computers, Inc.	DesignCAD 2D	Evolution Computing	EasyCAD
Amiable Technologies, Inc.	FlexiCAD	Evolution Computing	FastCAD
Archway Systems	PenDrafter	Evolution Computing	FastCAD 3D w/RenderMan
Ashlar Inc.	Vellum	Foresight Resources Corp.	Drafix CAD Ultra
Auto-Trol Technology Corp.	Jazzline	Foresight Resources Corp.	Drafix Windows CAD
auto.des.sys, Inc.	Form-Z	Forthought, Inc.	SNAP!
Autodesk Retail Products	AutoSketch (Windows)	Graphisoft	ArchiCAD
Autodesk Retail Products	Generic CADD	Graphsoft, Inc.	MiniCad+
Autodesk, Inc.	AutoCAD	IBM Corporation	IBM AES
c.a.s.a.GIFTS, Inc.	GIFTS	Intergraph Corp.	MicroStation
CADAM, Inc.	IBM CAD/Plus	International Microcomputer Software, Inc.	TurboCAD
cadcorp	wincad, 3D Studio, Microstation	ISICAD, Inc.	CADVANCE
Cadkey, Inc.	DataCAD	MegaCADD	MegaMODEL
CADMAX Corporation	CADMAX	Modern Computer-Aided Engineering, Inc.	INERTIA/InSolid
CADworks Inc.	Drawbase	Point Line U.S.A.	Point Line
Caroline Informatique	MTEL	Schroff	SilverScreen
CEDRA Corp.	The CEDRA System	Sigma Design, Inc	ARRIS
Computervision	CADDS5	StereoCAD, Inc.	REALTIME
Computervision	CYWare	STRATA, INC.	StrataVision 3D
Computervision	VersaCAD	Swanson Analysis Systems, Inc.	ANSYS FEA
Dassault Systems of America	Professional CADAM	UNIC, Inc.	Architrion II
Data Automation	DGS-2000	Wavefront Technologies, Inc.	The Advanced Visualizer
DesignCAD Inc.	DesignCAD 2D/3D Mac	Wiechers & Partner Datentechnik GmbH	LOGOCAD
Dickens Data Systems, Inc.	DesignBid		

MECHANICAL ALTER EGO: THE COMPUTER AS CYBERTOOL

At the beginning of the twenty-first century the number of software kits available to architects continues to proliferate exponentially. With no intention of being promotional or exhaustive, some of those now available are shown on the left.

The way that each of these packages, and the others that continue to appear constantly, are selected and used differs from firm to firm depending on design objectives and philosophy. Behnisch, Behnisch and Partner, led by scion Stefan Behnisch, defines one extreme of the position of using the computer as an adjunct to traditional design methods, and they have no intention of changing. Proclaiming with pride that "We are old fashioned when it comes to computers," Stefan explains that the firm instead relies heavily on physical models, using AutoCAD for repetitive drafting tasks and technical exploration. This results in a discernibly recursive pattern in concept development, as opposed to the singularity of each of the projects in a computer-led approach, for example Beachness by NOX (see p.142). In the North German State Clearing House Bank in Hannover, the combination of a low-rise datum surrounding a tower is the final stage in a series of evolutionary steps traceable in previous competition entries; the method of choice for the firm in obtaining many of their commissions. When it first appeared, in an earlier iteration, the tower had even more offsets than in its final realization at Hannover, but structural refinements and the learning curve relating to client acceptance of such a radical shift in the appearance of a well known typology changed the profile. Countless cardboard models led to the final composition; the structural possibilities were continually tested by computer.

The final configuration will certainly be recognizable on the city skyline, and sight lines to the complex also altered the profile. This alteration to conform to context, even if perceptual in this instance, is referred to as *situationarchitektur* by Stefan Behnisch, the literal English equivalent being less evocative than the German meaning of sensitive adaptation to a sense of place.

The Harbourside Centre Competition for a concert hall in Bristol, UK, which the firm won in 1996, but which unfortunately did not go ahead, helps define the term *situationarchitektur* – it is the credo of the firm – more clearly since in this case natural constraints are more in evidence. The competition project also underscores the preference for physical models validated or altered by digital investigation, which, in this instance, focused on acoustic performance and the envelope necessary to optimize it. The necessary dividing line between public processional and quiet performance space was intentionally exaggerated in the Bristol project, with a series of glass-enclosed promenades projecting in a fanned-out cantilever over the water of the harbor and the sound-sealed hall positioned on the landside behind it.

Although it was not built, the Bristol Concert Hall left an indelible impression, resulting in many requests by subsequent clients for similar kinds of formal expression, even though functions differed. The freedom and memorability of the forms in comparison to a more completely computer-generated project, such as the Dresden Cinema by Coop Himmelb(l)au (see pp.116–17), also raises the crucial issue of just how much a selected medium can enhance spatial experience. The Bristol Concert Hall seems to be an exception to the new, widely accepted assumption that computers can do it better.

Behnisch, Behnisch and Partner:
North German State Clearing Bank, Hannover
At present, clients still seem to relate more easily to
conventional site models, especially
in competitions.

Behnisch, Behnisch and Partner:
Bristol Harbourside Centre

Behnisch, Behnisch and Partner:
North German State Clearing Bank, Hannover
Physical models still provide a more viable method of assessing form for
many architects, and accurately convey formal interrelationships, unlike
computer renderings, in which shading can be deceptive.

Behnisch, Behnisch and Partner:
Bristol Harbourside Centre
Many architects only use computers for tedious, repetitive
tasks, as for this plan of the concert hall interior.

Behnisch, Behnisch and Partner:
Bristol Harbourside Centre
In descriptive diagrams, however, the computer often
brings new life to a functional chore.

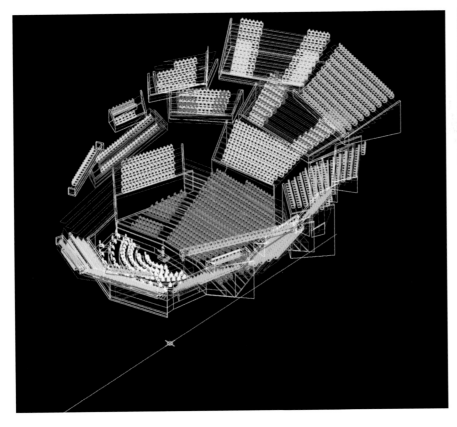

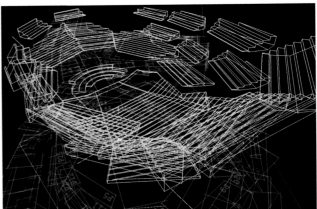

The way software is selected and applied differs substantially from firm to firm, depending on specialty, if any, the size of the project involved, design intent, and the particular personalities involved. NBBJ Architecture, for example, uses Silicon Graphics hardware, Alias/Wavefront three-dimensional visualization software, and Micro Station Trimforma three-dimensional documentation software to explore options with clients on a variety of large-scale projects in their various studios and then to study these in both electronic and physical site models.

NBBJ measures itself, at 800 strong, as the fifth largest architectural firm in the world, with 21 studios spread among six offices in the United States and projects in North and South America, Europe, and Asia. The design team of Peter Pran, Joey Myers, Jonathan Ward, and Jin Ah Park emphasizes that in their three-stage process of exploration, documentation, and implementation, a balance between virtual and physical reality is important to maintain a tactile handle on a project's progress. In the first stage, three-dimensional electronic information is used to create physical models; plexiglas and wood are laser cut and stereo-lithography (SLA) polymer resins are used to glue them together. In the working document phase isometric and axonometric drawings help contractors understand and scale components and details. The firm prides itself on carrying over three-dimensional electronic data from the exploratory design into the documentation stage, since they feel it increases accuracy, eliminates coordination problems, and helps to identify potential areas of difficulty early in the process, especially in taking sections through three-dimensional data for two-dimensional documentation. Alias/Wavefront software also allows the contractor to use this electronic data to manufacture full-scale parts of the final building, with far greater efficiency and accuracy.

Because it has offices in various cities and countries, NBBJ finds that Silicon Graphics specialized interactive software allows design teams to collaborate or discuss a project with a client,

since it has audio and video capability and allows them to sketch on screen at the same time, or to maneuver a computer model so that each participant can sketch over it. NBBJ also creates secure project-specific web pages to keep all involved parties informed.

Several projects help illustrate how NBBJ tries to use computer capability as a tool to differentiate themselves from other architects over a wide range of applications. The New York State Psychiatric Institute in New York City, completed between 1992 and 1998, is located on an especially fine urban site to the west of Riverside Drive.

Technology Builds Consensus

Simulation technology initially helped establish a configuration that would both ensure clear views from the building of the Hudson River, George Washington Bridge, and the northern end of Manhattan, as well as a low, six-story profile along Riverside Drive that would allow an open corridor from which the neighborhood around the Institute could still see the Hudson River. Because of the prominent location of the site – it is an entrance gateway to the city after crossing the George Washington Bridge – this capability was an invaluable design tool. It was also much easier to present to the numerous community groups and governmental officials that were involved in the project because of issues related to its highly visible location. The architects believe that the interactive capacity of the technology made it possible, in over 60 reviews, to change support for the project from less than 60 percent at the beginning of the design process to 98 percent, once all parties involved felt that they had direct involvement in changing various parts of it.

NBBJ: Seoul Dome
The large scale of sports facilities lends itself to bold forms.

Interjecting Fluidity

In the Graha Kuningan project, a 50-story tower designed
and built between 1995 and 1998 in the "golden triangle" in the
middle of Jakarta, Indonesia, NBBJ used the computer to
intentionally interject a discernible feeling of movement and fluidity
into a rigidly rectilinear urban core that was typical of post-war
development in South Asia. The computer was also invaluable in
helping to maximize usable floor area at 87 percent and to design
a core within a very tight area, leading to a double-decker elevator
system and a two-story "sky lobby" on the 34th and 35th floors.
The feeling of fluidity was achieved by two offset, gently curving
glass walls that are a foil to the minimalist, rectilinear core, and
which allow panoramic views at each level of the high rise, since it
is detailed to extend floor to floor. A roof terrace on the 47th floor
extends out to intentionally disrupt the clean sweep of the glass
curve, as do portions of a five-story base that houses restaurants,
retail space, a theater, and a bank, providing a total
of 1.5 million square feet (138,000 square meters) of office,
retail, and entertainment facilities in the second tallest building
in Jakarta.

   NBBJ remained heavily involved in the urban expansion in Asia
that came to a grinding halt with the economic crash of 1998
to 1999, but which is now slowly returning. The most prominent
projects in the region from that period are the El Presidente
Apartment and Office Tower in Makati near Manila, the Philippines;
the Central Business District of Manila (1997); the Seoul Dome
at the LG Twins Baseball Stadium, Korea (1997–8); and the Kwan
Tong Town Centre in Hong Kong (1998).

NBBJ: Seoul Dome
Digital renderings have continued the "paper architecture" tradition
of the 1980s, in which graphics became an end in themselves.

High-Tech Communications Wrapped
in an Ancient Metaphor

NBBJ relied heavily on symbolism to write the disparate parts of
the enormous new sports complex in Seoul: a 43,000-seat, multi-
purpose baseball stadium for the LG Group that will also
showcase the 2002 World Cup Soccer Games. In addition to the
stadium, the complex brief includes public concourse levels,
cinemas, restaurants, an entertainment facility, an exhibition hall,
health club, banquet facilities, department and retail stores, and a
three-level parking garage. An all-encompassing roof, representing
the hospitality of the people of Seoul and their welcome to visitors,
unites these interweaving functions which can each be accessed
by using an electronic debit card. Configured into a tube-like
structure, this roof breaks into "arms" that "embrace" the stadium
at the center of the complex, the split also symbolizing the two
firms that joined to become the LG Group. Alias/Wavefront three-
dimensional visualization software helped the designers configure
the curved metal roof, which they wanted to seem to move
"forcefully upwards, articulating a spirited sense of endlessness."

Just prior to the relocation of the Hong Kong International
Airport to Chek Lap Kok, a NBBJ team comprising Jim Jonassen,
Peter Pran as Design Principal, Dorman Anderson, Jonathan Ward,
Joey Myers, Duncan Griffin, and Hideto Tanaka completed Kwan
Tong Town Centre, just a few blocks away, in 1998. Bounded by
Mutwah Street to the northwest, Hip Wo Street to the east and
Kwan Tong Road to the south, the site was planned to
accommodate an 88-story office tower and a 43-story office
tower, five residential tower blocks, of which two are 65 stories,
two 43 stories, and one 19 stories high; a 14-story hotel; and
1.6 million square feet (145,000 square meters) of retail space,
surrounding a large pedestrian atrium. While the towers would
have been too high when the old International Airport was in
operation, the team planned for an easing of height restrictions
after transition and used simulation alternatives to decide on
the most desirable skyline profile and shading patterns, and
connection to a large gently sloping Central People's Plaza.
The Centre, which includes a below-grade bus terminal and
connections to an MTR station, is intended to become a generator
of future development in Kowloon, and a model for the future.

NBBJ: Seoul Dome

The connection between cyberarchitecture and modernism is evident in aerial, axonometric views, which objectify the building in question.

NBBJ: Kwan Tong Town Centre, Hong Kong
The preference for skyscrapers throughout Asia has been fed by
glossy computer renderings, which accentuate their appeal.

NBBJ: Kwan Tong Town Centre, Hong Kong
Glass has always been difficult to render with traditional
graphics, but now can be shown quite realistically.

Issues of Difference

The Kwan Tong Town Centre highlights several important issues
raised in the Introduction about space, cultural differentiation, and
the dangers of technological insensitivity to these variations. The
question here becomes the extent to which that blindness would
still exist, whether the computer was the predominant design tool
or not. Towers and residential tower blocks are ubiquitous
throughout Asia – a pragmatic solution generally accepted as a
result of the massive pressures of need, tight schedules, land
scarcity, and the cost of real estate. And so, with its vertical
emphasis, Kwan Tong is business as usual, which seems to be a
lost opportunity to break the regimented pattern that now exists
in the region and therefore make a difference. The same may be
said for the central "atrium." The evidence of the speed of
homogeneous globalization is nowhere more evident than in the
proliferation of Western mall-like spaces throughout an area of the
world that has no established tradition of public space, such as
plazas or piazzas, in the European sense.

Nature Surrounds a City Within

NBBJ is on firmer ideological ground in Oslo, with the design of a
new headquarters for Telenor on the site of the Oslo International
Airport at Farnebu (relocated to Gardemoen in 1998). Telenor is
the largest telecommunications company in Norway, a country that
is among the world leaders in the information revolution. As with
Toyo Ito's Mediatheque in Sendai, Japan, this is an instance of an
architect having the chance to represent electronic technology
with the same media. The memory of an airport runway ending
near a spectacular overview of the Oslo Fjord adds the *frisson* of
the machine in a natural paradise. In addition to Peter Pran as
Design Principal, the competition winning team in this instance
included Scott Wyatt as Partner in Charge, and designers Joseph
Herrin, Joey Myers, Jin Ah Park, Curtis Wagner, and Jonathan
Ward. They devised a two-phase 2.2 million square foot (207,000
square meter) complex to accommodate 6,000 staff members.
This "office for the future" is more like a small city, and is aligned
along the axis of the old runway, directing views toward the fjord.
Two curved "boulevards" organized along this axis define a main
entrance leading to a "plaza" at the heart of the complex, with an
arrival hall and information and education center that serves as an
orientation point for visitors – a place where the inside and
outside worlds can mix. True to their name, the boulevards are
treated as internal "streets," with cafes, restaurants, and shops en
route to the central reception areas for each of the eight office
wings. Following the trend in such electronic cities, these wings
were conceived as democratic, non-hierarchical, and free, to foster
interaction and variation. The basic office units, arranged in groups
from two to six, are joined by bridges and recreation areas for use
during work breaks. This clustering allows for as many as 700
people to interact in each area, and once again the idea of an
"atrium" is used; in this case they are placed between the wings
as extensions of the "plaza" and "boulevards," as places for
interaction between each of the eight office extensions. The sheer
scale of this enterprise is staggering: the designers have used a
different number of floors, and a variation of views and internal
modular arrangements to give each wing an individual identity.

NBBJ: Telenor headquarters, Oslo
Self-sufficiency is a new trend in office environments,
resulting in complexes that resemble small towns.

NBBJ: Telenor headquarters, Oslo
Corridors in the new self-contained office blocks are
treated like interior streets.

Back in the United States, NBBJ used their computer
capability to sculpt the surface of Vulcan Northwest, a speculative
office and retail tower in Seattle, to respond to three contextual
elements: the Space Needle at the opposite end of Second
Avenue, Pioneer Square adjacent to the site, and the pedestrian-
oriented business area called the International District, to the east.
A tilted silicone-jointed glass window wall curves toward the
entrance on the north, facing the Space Needle and the skyline of
downtown Seattle, while the dynamic movement of automobiles
and trains on the western side is interpreted by the singular
sweep of a curtain wall shaped like a parallelogram, which wraps
around the northwest corner of the building, as if sliding along its
surface. The parallelogram, which begins at the fourth floor,
cantilevers out four feet and leans outward at a four-degree angle
toward the street, reaching the property line at parapet level. Many
details reinforce this impression of movement. While the glass wall
has no vertical mullions, it has horizontal dividers of differing
profiles, with some mullion ends, or caps, actually disappearing
behind the glass, blurring the visual perception of inside and
outside and making the curtain wall seem to undulate. The

precision required to achieve details such as this would be
extremely difficult to achieve without computer technology. The
east façade, facing the International District, relates to pedestrian
scale with carved precast planes, separated by a vertical strip of
glass at the entrance, formed into a box that seems to be
exploding from the impact of Second Avenue intersecting it.

The International District and Pioneer Square are home to
Union Station and King Street Station, respectively – historic
reminders that Seattle was once the only city in the United States
where two competing train stations were located next to each
other. Union Station has subsequently been converted into offices
for Sound Transit, the headquarters for a light rail system in the
future. NBBJ has chosen to recall this heritage of movement
figuratively rather than literally, using the most advanced
technology now available to capture the spirit of the technological
achievements of the past. They were further prompted by the
knowledge that their client had also commissioned CATIA maestro
Frank Gehry, featured in Chapter 2, to design the Experience
Music Project in the same city.

NBBJ: Vulcan Northwest, Seattle
A high profile site called for a new landmark
in Seattle.

NBBJ: Vulcan Northwest, Seattle
The sense of movement in the façade of the Vulcan
headquarters was inspired by the Union and King Street
Railway stations nearby.

RoTo: Hollywood-Orange development, Los Angeles
RoTo uses the computer to extract objective information about
a project, before starting design.

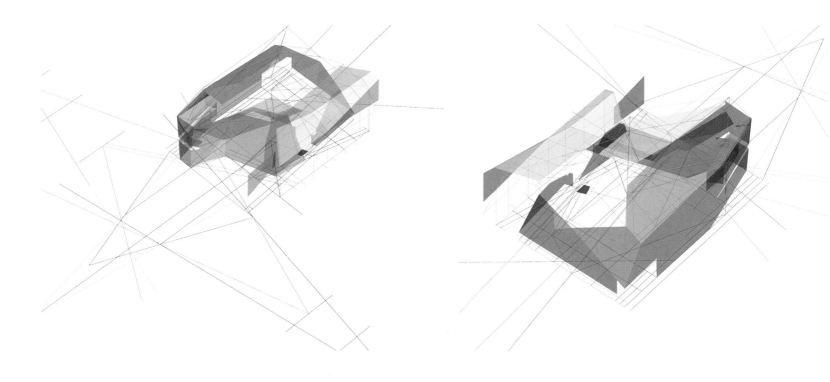

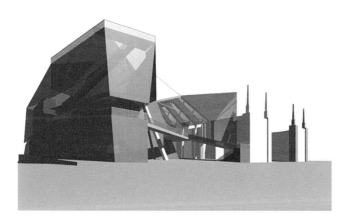

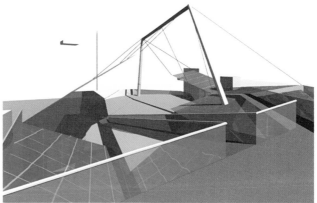

RoTo: Hollywood-Orange development, Los Angeles
Constant pedestrian and automobile traffic along Hollywood
Boulevard were a strong incentive to use the building as a billboard.

RoTo: Hollywood-Orange development, Los Angeles
Sequential diagrams allowed the architects to coordinate structural
framing with the most prominent sight lines.

RoTo Reinvents Hollywood

At a smaller scale, RoTo Architects, a relatively small firm of six
permanent professional staff – with Michael Rotondi and Clark
Stevens as principals and Brian Reiff as associate – use computer
capability in a somewhat similar way, though on a smaller scale,
working back and forth between physical and simulation models in
the search for form. Michael Rotondi is one of the founders of the
Southern California Institute of Architecture (SCI-Arc), where he
served as director from 1987 to 1997. Along with then partner
Thom Mayne, Rotondi also co-founded the Los Angeles-based
firm Morphosis in 1976 before going on to create RoTo with
Morphosis alumnus Clark Stevens in 1991. In spite of RoTo's
intentionally circumscribed size – it has been kept small so that its
members can relate more effectively to each other and to clients
– the firm has received international acclaim for its sensitive,
unconventional approach to a number of diverse projects.

It is an ironic coincidence that RoTo has employed virtual
reality in their search for a way to revive Hollywood, the paradigm
of superficiality. Now known in Los Angeles as the thoroughfare
which best exemplifies Gertrude Stein's axiom of having "no there,
there," Hollywood Boulevard has undoubtedly seen better days, but
still has such a powerful mystique that it continues to draw more
than six million tourists a year. At its zenith in the 1920s Hollywood
Boulevard attracted crowds to glamorous movie houses, exclusive
hotels, and restaurants frequented by stars who worked at studios
along the strip and lived nearby in the hills above Whitley Terrace.
Seedy bookstores and clubs at the other end of the social
spectrum provided a compelling mixture of flashy spectacle and
the forbidden. The combination of the superficially grand and
glaringly vulgar, which now draws so many to Las Vegas, made it a
legend because the unexpected could and often did happen there.
It had a mixture of what Michael Rotondi has called "public spaces
in private places," that gave it vitality and mystery, a backdrop
against which fantasy could be acted out, a microcosm of a city
built on that desire.

The Hollywood Freeway, completed in 1954, was the first of
several death knells, cutting diagonally across Whitley Terrace and
separating the residences of the rich in the hills above from the
Boulevard below. Then the film and television studios moved to
more spacious, easily accessed locations in the 1970s and 1980s,
taking away the lifeblood of the Boulevard. Its vitality soon became
a memory, marked only by a few remaining artifacts like Mann's
Chinese Theater. But the legend is so strong that tourists from all
over the world still come in search of the ineffable glamour that
once reigned here, in an attempt to alleviate the pervasive
sameness of consumer culture. The prospect of capitalizing on
that yearning has prompted a proposal for a large entertainment
complex next door to the Chinese Theater to include 14 theaters,
a hotel, and a new venue for the Academy Awards, all expected to
cost in excess of $300 million, three times the initial expense of
Universal City Walk.

RoTo: Hollywood-Orange development, Los Angeles
The Chinese Theater (on the right of the picture), which has
come to symbolize the heyday of Hollywood glamour, was one
of the most important influences for RoTo.

Keen to take advantage of the commercial potential offered by six million tourists a year, the Hollywood-Orange Land Group, who own the lot at the corner of Hollywood Boulevard and Orange Drive, involved RoTo in a project which the firm appropriately calls Hollywood-Orange. From the beginning, the developers placed an emphasis on flat surfaces for billboards: advertising could bring them significant revenue considering the weight of pedestrian and automobile traffic along the busy Boulevard and the crowds that visit Mann's Chinese. The brief included four new theaters, two levels of retail space, a restaurant, a public plaza, and parking.

Neutral Mapping or a Genetic Urban Code

RoTo did not introduce Power CAD and Form-Z to the Hollywood-Orange project until the client's requirements had first been organized with conventional bubble diagrams and conceptual sketches. The programs were then used in a process that Rotondi describes as "reading and redescribing the site, to provide a neutral mapping, so that the building begins to reflect all the things around it." Once Form-Z was used to model the concept sketches into three-dimensional planes, information about the surrounding context was also continuously refined, and physical models were built to confirm and clarify the forms that emerged on the computer screen. The designers feel that these models, along with continuous sketching, were invaluable as a parallel method of trial and error that helped to adjust proportions and refine details. The models were used up to and during the final stages, along with the computer renderings, which the architects feel are more easily understood by the client and members of the public in all presentations.

In spite of RoTo's belief that Power CAD and Form-Z were used as tools in a neutral mapping process, the radical formal change evident in the series of schematic models – where an increasingly planar configuration appears – shows the power of the medium to redirect form. In this instance the excavation of a "genetic urban code" led to several specific strategies. One of these was for a thin circulation spine to connect Hollywood Boulevard on the south with a tourist bus drop-off point on the north, creating a gallery that would bisect the site and become a lobby for the theaters. This axis gradually moved eastward, as the building took on the appearance of a positive solid mass, with negative circulation space carved out of it. The entrance loggia began as a simple rectangular corridor, but computer diagrams helped to discover a central balance point at which all edges converged, and the equality of entrance cones in the diagram, on both the north and south edges of the site, suggested a building with no front or back.

The computer-generated lines of force diagram also helped to locate a central lobby on axis with the side entrance to the elliptical atrium of the Chinese Theater, allowing the client to sell tickets to the four theaters in Hollywood-Orange and a fifth in the atrium, and also establish a symbolic connection between new and old. The circular form of the lobby was accentuated to reflect the curve of the elliptical atrium and reinforce this connection. These intersecting lines were based on the geometric center of the lot and a tower was designated at this point to mark its importance. The intersecting lines indicated a triangle that remained a guideline for the shape of the building throughout consecutive design stages, and the geometrical associations given by computer established a prototypical grid that then organized the skewed, asymmetrical planes of each façade, as well as helping to determine the most important cones of vision along the Boulevard that would help locate perpendicular planes for billboards. Computer studies also pointed to a framed view between the edges of the Roosevelt Hotel and Bank of America building, which remained an important determinant as the design progressed.

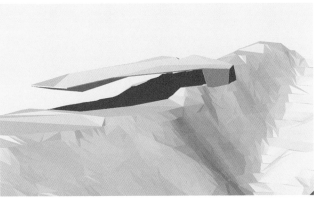

RoTo: Xiyuan Buddhist Monastery, Los Angeles
Architect and client collaborated closely in making calmness
manifest in the union between architecture and nature.

RoTo: Oak Pass house, Los Angeles
The coordinated use of physical and computer modeling made
it possible to carefully fit this house into its hilly site.

The four theaters were eventually removed from the project,
but the idea of the front to back spine remained viable, as a
playful processional way between two stories that would help
return the sense of spectacle to Hollywood Boulevard. The design
was then driven by the inclusion of ramps, bridges, and stairs, and
by the idea of a grand semi-enclosed roof terrace and a
crystalline, transparent, planar glass skin to make interior and
exterior movement more visible. In its final form, Hollywood-
Orange is a multifaceted glass volume on which the visual
interplay between transparency and opacity has been used as a
subtle optical strategy to imply an upward spiral of solids and
voids. This is played out against the horizontal datum of a soaring,
covered loggia that invites people in, and against the visual
emphasis of signage. The structure's crystal image symbolizes
its function of reflecting everything around it, made possible
by computer.

In the Xiyuan Buddhist Monastery and Oak Pass residence
projects, RoTo have adopted a similar strategy of initial graphic
investigation, computer simulation of conceptual sketches, and
contextual mapping, which is used to inform and possibly redirect
initial intuitive responses. This is combined with extensive physical
modeling to reach a final synthesis of graphic, digital, and three-
dimensionally modeled discovery. The Oak Pass house especially
underscores this interplay. Nestled in a canyon, the house is
likened by Rotondi to an "Albert Frey cave," in reference to the
penchant of that modernist – whose influence among certain
architects in Los Angeles extends far beyond a relatively limited
body of work – to fuse minimal steel and glass enclosures to
natural forms, such as boulders. The computer-assisted
topographic model indicated a triangular cluster of critical high
points, one of which was shaved off to ease access to two levels
cascading down a canyon wall. These are covered with an
undulating, folded shell, a new phenomenon reinterpreted by
Form-Z, which in this case has replaced the human-made genetic
code of Hollywood with a natural genetic code. Rotondi sees this
folded shell as being emblematic of the paradigm shift that
computer-aided design has wrought – from the formal articulation
of points in the 1970s and 1980s, to planes.

RoTo: Oak Pass house, Los Angeles
Longitudinal sections illustrate the extent to which
the house has been carved into the ground.

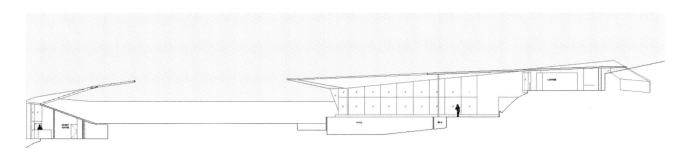

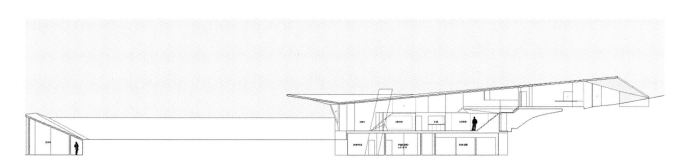

Morphosis: Diamond Ranch High School, Pomona
Morphosis has used the characteristics of what many others would
consider to be an unbuildable site to best advantage.

Morphosis: Diamond Ranch High School, Pomona
Complete conversion from conventional drafting to computers,
long before others did so, shows a courageous commitment to
digital technology in a firm known for its strong design orientation.

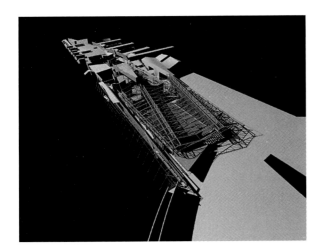

Morphosis Makes the Earth Move

The natural landscape played an equally important role in arch-
rival Morphosis' solution to the challlenge posed by a steeply
sloping 72-acre (30-hectare) site overlooking Pomona, California.
Landed with what many considered to be unbuildable terrain in
exchange for a favourable financial consideration too attractive to
refuse, Morphosis' School District client was fortunate in having an
architectural firm that is undaunted by such monumental
challenges. Here, the obstacles included slopes that vary from 1:1
to 5:1, resulting in a 380-foot (115-meter) drop across the entire
site, and local cut-and-fill regulations that did not allow moving
earth from or to the site, or new slopes in excess of 2:1, to prevent
uncontrolled storm water drainage and erosion.

Using these restrictions to best advantage, Thom Mayne
and senior designer John Endicott distributed this 150,000 square
foot (14,000 square meter) public high school – including 50
classrooms and laboratories, a gymnasium, a library, a cafeteria,
administration offices, and 770 parking spaces – along a retaining
wall extended across the site, preserving existing oak trees and
native grasses as much as possible. This allowed the leveling of
the upper slope to accommodate three soccer fields and one
football field, two baseball diamonds, seven tennis, eight
basketball, and four volleyball courts, and another extensive
parking area.

Morphosis: Diamond Ranch High School, Pomona
Classrooms project out over an earth-bermed retaining wall
that runs across the site.

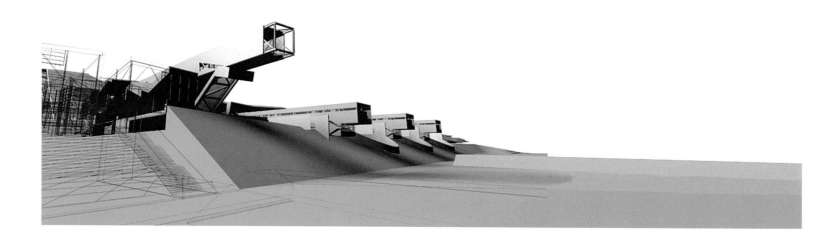

By housing each grade year in an individual linear bar building, and projecting each building over a battered retaining wall perpendicular to the shared administrative dining and sports activities above, Morphosis was able to create courts between the buildings, giving each grade year a sense of identity. This arrangement also allowed the top of each wing to be used as a roof terrace for watching outdoor events, as well as for enjoying the region's fine weather and the spectacular view of the Pomona skyline. The library occupies part of a fourth, extended bar.

Besides facilitating a logical arrangement, this epic landscape strategy has also proven to be very efficient, packing a very complex brief into less than half the available site. The close integration between the high school and the slope is intentionally contrasted with a palette of materials that sets the human-made against the natural setting. The school is constructed of steel-braced frames − which allow the cantilevering of the classroom

ranks over the retaining wall, precast concrete decking, and *in situ* cast concrete for the retaining wall. Exterior walls are either concrete or sheet metal.

Thom Mayne was one of the first top-ranking architects to fully commit to computer-aided design, banishing parallel rules and triangles from his office before many others took the leap. Considering Mayne's intensive hands-on design approach, this shift is especially impressive, but it has not discernibly changed his direction, since he has also continued to rely on intuitive conceptualization in the initial stage, as well as on the extensive use of physical study and presentation models. Because of the scale of the natural challenges presented at Diamond Ranch, completed in early 2000, the project best exemplifies Mayne's balanced integration of a highly individualized design approach and the use of digital data gathering to make the assimilation of complex information more manageable.

Morphosis: Diamond Ranch High School, Pomona
The concept of building the site takes on new meaning in this epic earth-moving achievement.

Morphosis: Diamond Ranch High School, Pomona
The classrooms have a crystalline, geological quality that ties them to the land.

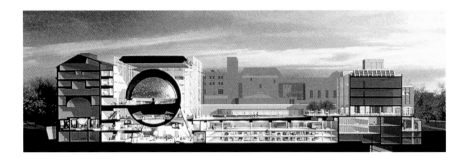

**Polshek Partnership: Rose Center for Earth
and Space, New York**
Every effort has been made to have the Rose Center
planetarium fit into its surroundings.

The Universe Is a Sphere Floating above Manhattan

The capabilities of the computer as a design tool are also amply
demonstrated in the new Rose Center for Earth and Space
(Hayden Plantarium) at the American Museum of Natural History
in Manhattan, by the James Stewart Polshek Partnership, which
opened in January 2000. The spherical planetarium, which is 87
feet (26.5 meters) in diameter and can accommodate 585 visitors,
seems to float inside a giant glass cube, with no visible top,
bottom, or side supports. The skin of the sphere is made up of
5,599,663 lozenge-shaped acoustical pieces. Each piece differs
according to curvature, and could never have been detailed, drawn,
manufactured, or constructed manually, making this a feat that
would not have been possible without digital applications. Polshek
says the sphere was inspired by the cross section of the old
Hayden Planetarium, built in 1935, which had a copper dome 75
feet (23 meters) in diameter. CAD made the concept legible for
the client in ways that conventional representation never could,
doubling its singularity, since it would not be possible without
renderings that attracted donors and pacified neighborhood
groups. Wireframe outlines helped determine shading patterns,
which were later tracked by animation, and computer studies
predicted temperature and lighting levels, which were eventually
sent by e-mail to the fabricator of the skin panels in Los Angeles.

The sphere's apparent levitation is an optical illusion, since a
steel tripod supports a circular truss on which the upper half of
the sphere rests and from which the lower half is suspended.
The 432-seat Space Theater, which uses a Zeiss video projection
to reproduce the night sky on the dome overhead, occupies the
upper half of the hemisphere, while 150 viewers stand on a circular
platform to watch a recreation of the beginning of the universe in
the Big Bang Theater below. Both theaters are reached by a 320-
foot-(97.5-meter-) long spiral ramp which is also a testament to
cybernetic assistance, since its constantly changing dimensions
would have been a nightmare to design using conventional
representation. To achieve a transparent, crystalline appearance,
the glass wall panels of the enveloping cube have no mullions, and
are supported by stainless steel "spiders" connected to tension
rods projecting from a steel wall truss.

A Virtual Simulation of the Cosmos

The Planetarium is primarily a public institution, and as such relies
on the same interactive, personal discovery that has transformed
the design of museums internationally. The ramp doesn't just
access the theaters, it is a "Cosmic Pathway" that also explains
the unfolding of time from the Big Bang to the present. A square
walkway, supported at the equatorial position by the same truss
from which the sphere is suspended, forms the "Scale of the
Universe," by which visitors can measure the size of the Milky Way
galaxy against the size of the earth, sun, and other planets in the
solar system. A bridge, which penetrates to the center of the
sphere, becomes the gateway from the real world into a virtually
described universe, presented to viewers in spaceship-like seats
that rumble through a teleologically straight "ride" to distant
galaxies that doesn't yet take refinement on the theory of General
Relativity or String theory into consideration. But the universe it
describes is a revelation, since Hayden Planetarium scientists, like
the architects, have also taken maximum advantage of computer
technology to achieve the previously impossible. By loading
information from as many sources as possible, but primarily from
the Hubble telescope, they have been able to virtually model or
simulate parts of the universe, allowing them to be experienced
three-dimensionally for the first time. The seven lenses of the
Zeiss star projector can be used to reconstruct various pathways,
and as new data are continually added, the sky becomes an
increasingly important tool with which astronomers can model
events that are millions of light years away.

Polshek Partnership: Rose Center for Earth and Space, New York
A spiraling ramp allows the vast interior of the planetarium to be slowly revealed.

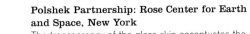

Polshek Partnership: Rose Center for Earth and Space, New York
The transparency of the glass skin accentuates the spherical and cubic volumes at dusk.

Foster and Partners: Greater London Authority
The implementation of complex geometries made possible by computer is especially evident in the recent projects of the Foster Partnership.

Foster and Partners: Greater London Authority
New configurations have presented contractors and manufacturers with new challenges, affecting the entire construction industry.

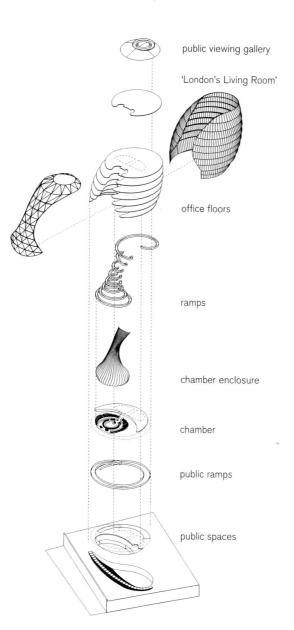

public viewing gallery

'London's Living Room'

office floors

ramps

chamber enclosure

chamber

public ramps

public spaces

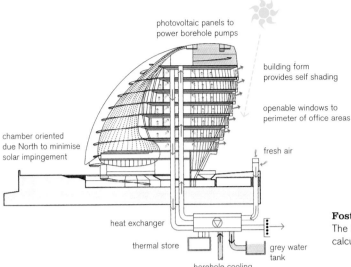

photovoltaic panels to
power borehole pumps

building form
provides self shading

openable windows to
perimeter of office areas

chamber oriented
due North to minimise
solar impingement

fresh air

heat exchanger

thermal store

grey water
tank

borehole cooling

Foster and Partners: Greater London Authority
The impact of environmental forces is much easier to
calculate and building envelopes have changed accordingly.

Environmentally Modeled Democratic Transparency

When designing the Greater London Authority Assembly Building,
Sir Norman Foster and Partners also chose a sphere, in this case
for environmental reasons – since it has 25 percent less surface
area than a cube of the same volume – to reduce heat gain and
loss. To achieve optimum performance, the pure geometrical form
has been manipulated almost exclusively through computer testing
by the London office of the structural services and acoustical
engineers Ove Arup and Partners. The form of this and other
recent structures by Foster and Partners differs markedly from
that of their most notable designs of the past, such as the Hong
Kong and Shanghai Bank. The curvilinear sleekness of these
recent projects is entirely a function of an increasingly reliance on
CAD. As with their conceptual approach to the new Reichstag in
Berlin, Foster's office also sought to use transparency in the GLA
scheme to both symbolize and facilitate a more democratic
governmental process, to allow Londoners to see their elected
assembly in action as well as to provide spectacular views for the
people working in the building. The site is adjacent to Tower
Bridge and directly opposite the Tower of London, so these views
are mainly directed at St. Paul's Cathedral. As at the Rose Center
for Earth and Space, a broad spiraling ramp will also provide the
main means of access to all ten levels of the 185,000-square-foot
(17,000-square-meter) Headquarters. The 200-seat Assembly
Chamber is the principal space – rising up through the center of
the entire building inside a wrapper of offices for members and

their administrative staff – and it presented the acousticians with
a particularly difficult contingency. The attitude of accessibility
culminates on the ninth floor, in a flexible public space that the
architects have optimistically labeled "London's Living Room."
The rooftop, which offers stunning views across the city, is open
to the public and will be available for a range of activities from
exhibitions to social events of up to 200 people. At its base, the
GLA is carved into the river terrace. The ground floor houses
committee rooms that overlook a protected open, stepped
parterre, and also have access to a public café at ground-floor
level. All nine floors share a central service core.

The unilateral attitude toward accessibility at the GLA was
balanced against view and environmental requirements – the
orientation required for maximum solar gain in winter and shade in
summer has been achieved while still making the building
intentionally omnidirectional as far as entrance is concerned.
When complete the Authority building will be the final set piece in
a chain of landmarks along the south bank of the Thames in
Southwark, from the Design Museum, H.M.S. *Belfast*, and
Southwark Cathedral to the Globe Theatre and the new Tate
Modern at Bankside. This sequence is further enhanced by the
impressive string of new Underground stations along the Jubilee
Line Extension that connects the sites to the rest of London.

Foster and Partners: Swiss Re headquarters, London
The press have made unexpected metaphorical comparisons with
the unusual shape of the tower.

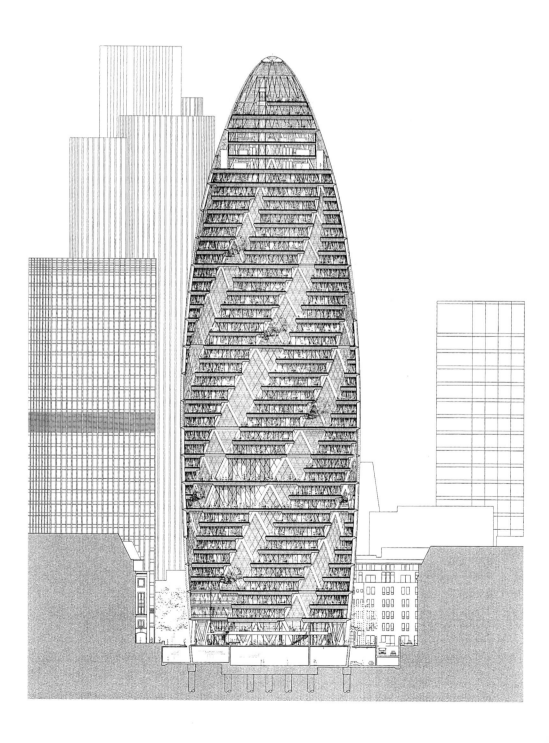

Foster and Partners: Swiss Re headquarters, London
Top: The prime location of the Swiss Re headquarters, in the heart
of the City of London, ensures it will always have pedestrian activity
around the perimeter.

Bottom: Taking advantage of a loophole in height restrictions, the
new tower will undoubtedly change the skyline of London.

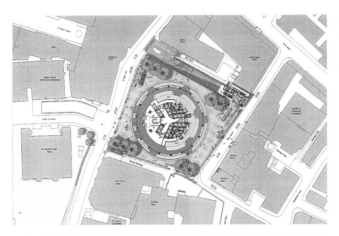

Swiss Re-ascendant

The Swiss Reinsurance Company, founded in Zurich in 1863, and
now the 41st largest company in Europe, has operations in more
than 30 countries, employing about 9,000 people, with six
separate locations within the City of London alone. As the second
largest global insurance group, the company needed to establish a
high-visibility London headquarters in the city's financial center.
Swiss Reinsurance has a record of owning and commissioning
environmentally progressive buildings, and they selected a site that
was able to accommodate a tall building. These factors made it
possible for Foster and Partners to implement contextual and
sustainable principles on a large scale.

Bounded by St. Mary Axe, Bury Street, Bury Court, and Browns
Buildings, in the heart of the City, the Swiss Re site is free of the
height constraints imposed on most of the remainder of the
financial district, implemented to conserve the view corridors of St.
Paul's and the Great Fire Monument. Within the perimeter of a
cluster of high-rises grouped around Tower 42, the International
Financial Centre, the site has a continuous pedestrian route
around its boundary, does not lie in a conservation area, and has
no underground conditions that would prohibit the construction of
a skyscraper.

All of these factors prompted Foster to make a proposal which
he has described as "radical – socially, technically, architecturally,
and spatially." The social reference presumably relates to the 590-
foot (179.8-meter) height of the seductively curved tower in a city
which, aside from the purely pragmatic and supremely ugly British
Telecom tower, has discouraged vertical expression and
exploration. The technical breakthrough, which also encompasses
architectural and spatial innovations, is a diagonally braced
structure with an acoustical buffer, creating an aerodynamic form
that drives natural ventilation because of the large pressure
differentials that are generated, pulling in fresh, outside air at

Foster and Partners: Music Centre, Gateshead
A curving shell encloses three performance spaces of various sizes that are intended to transform the cultural life of Tyneside in northeast England.

Foster and Partners: Music Centre, Gateshead
The new Music Centre is the culmination of a long planning process meant to provide the Newcastle area with more entertainment options.

every floor level through horizontal slots in the glass and aluminum skin. This diagonal frame also generates the rotation of each of 40 successive floors, so that voids at the edge of each floor plate form a segment of a series of upwardly spiraling atria, which contribute to natural ventilation through stack effect. Though not intended to eliminate the need for air-conditioning altogether, this naturally induced ventilation will supplement it and therefore lower running costs are projected. The atria are alternated with a suspended garden at every sixth floor, to help control airflow and provide the required fire compartments. The gardens also oxygenate the air, helping to purify the interior microclimate just outside the offices.

The visual interaction that is promoted by the spiraling floors and open atria is another aspect of the radical social change to which Foster refers, and is considered an improvement on the relatively compartmentalized sequestering of employees on stacked floors in the Hong Kong and Shanghai Bank, in spite of the atrium also used there. The perceived need to improve such interaction is further testimony to the pervasiveness of the "cities within" syndrome frequently referred to here, although it is difficult to imagine digital sweat-shops or cyber mosh pits of the Los Angeles variety in a sleek, high-tech tower in London.

Visual interaction is one thing, meaningful social contact is another. It remains to be seen if promotional promises of humane spaces can survive the considerable demands of corporate image. Concerns expressed about the "public realm" and "townscape" around the base of the tower acknowledge the problems of scale that are caused by a skyscraper, and every effort has been made to "animate" what has so often become a windswept concrete wasteland in contemporary experience. To ameliorate this effect the architects have added low stone walls that can double as seating, an instant copse of mature trees in planters, and a chic new glass and stone six-story café bar at the Bury Street corner.

There is also a kiosk at the north-west side of the site and a shop in the minimally enclosed base of the tower — all intended to create an attractive space for public use.

Cultural Turbine on Tyneside

Swiss Re — as vertical generator of natural ventilation in the City of London — has been followed by a formal equivalent on Tyneside, near Newcastle, which is meant to whip up a tornado of cultural activity there. The new Music Centre at Gateshead, which had been in the planning stage for over a decade before Foster was selected, is a third, startling example of the stylistic change that an increasing use of CAD has brought at Foster and Partners. Intended to provide culture-starved locals, who must travel long distances to hear larger folk and jazz, ensembles, or chamber music and concerts, with a more convenient venue, the Centre will also undoubtedly be a highly visible landmark that will regenerate the Tyne riverfront, since it is expected that half a million visitors will patronize it yearly.

An enveloping, shell-like carapace encloses three main performance spaces; a large 1,650-seat hall for concerts; a smaller, more flexible, 400-seat room for folk, jazz and chamber music; and a third rehearsal hall for a new Regional Music School that is intended to establish a regional and international reputation for musical education. Curved terraces inside the shell serve all three halls and focus views toward the Tyne and the Newcastle skyline. The largest of these terraces has been treated as an interior concourse — directly connected to main entrances on the east and west — that leads directly to the box office and information centre, past cafés, bars, and shops along the way. The Music School is below this concourse and the foyers for each of the three halls are above it. Entertainment facilities, backstage dressing, costume spaces, and green rooms and administrative offices are on the south side of the building.

Foster and Partners: Music Centre, Gateshead
A large terrace overlooking the Tyne has been enclosed
to become the main concourse off the Centre.

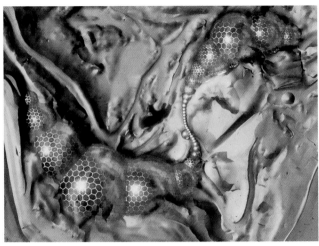

Nicholas Grimshaw & Partners: Eden Project Visitor Centre, Cornwall
A landscape pockmarked by abandoned tin mines has been transformed into a facility to raise public awareness of ecology.

Nicholas Grimshaw & Partners: Eden Project Visitor Centre, Cornwall
A flexible, glass-enclosed frame allows the Eden ecosystems to freely adapt to the crevices created by mining in the past.

Eden in Cornwall

The emphasis on computer generation evident in these latest projects to come out of Foster's office seems to be a logical extension of a continual commitment to avant-garde technology, especially as it applies to the cause of a more contextual interrelationship with architecture and an increasingly proactive concern about the environment.

Other proponents of the clearly identifiable British direction led by Norman Foster and Richard Rogers – grouped under the rubric "High-Tech," which they both dislike – have also followed this trend. Another notable recent example is the Eden Project, opened 2000, by the Nicholas Grimshaw & Partners. Located in Cornwall, southwest England, it takes advantage of abandoned pit mines in what was once one of the world's biggest tin-producing areas by reclaiming the scarred earth for a research center that will study ways to save it. Arguably in the same genre as Biosphere II and III built in the desert in the American Southwest, so named and numbered because the earth was prosaically considered to be Biosphere I, the Eden Project also aims to replicate the majority of the earth's ecosystems under a hermetically sealed glass shell. But the Cornwall enterprise differs in one significant respect. While both environmental replicas have been backed by entrepreneurs whose intentions have not been entirely altruistic, since they both hope to reap financial benefits from research findings, the Eden enclosure will be open to the public – a glass-wrapped earth in microcosm, packaged as a theme park. In the American scenario, rigorously trained Bionauts were locked inside the glorified greenhouse until hydroponically induced irritability brought the communal experiment to an abrupt halt. The complex section of the cascading, artificial Eden, and the intricate folds of its glass panels, made computer assistance a necessity in its design, which once again would have been nearly impossible by conventional means.

There is also considerable, ironic poetry in this cybernetically formed new Eden, intended to supplant the natural original. It is an artificial twenty-first-century utopia created in virtual space, on a par with the human genome project and other Biotech initiatives as a replacement exercise carried out at the most fundamental level of life.

Nicholas Grimshaw & Partners: Eden Project
Visitor Centre, Cornwall
A different formal language distinguishes the reception
center (foreground) from the glass-enclosed halls.

**Nicholas Grimshaw & Partners: Eden Project
Visitor Centre, Cornwall**
The "exoskeleton" is as biomorphic as the plants it protects.

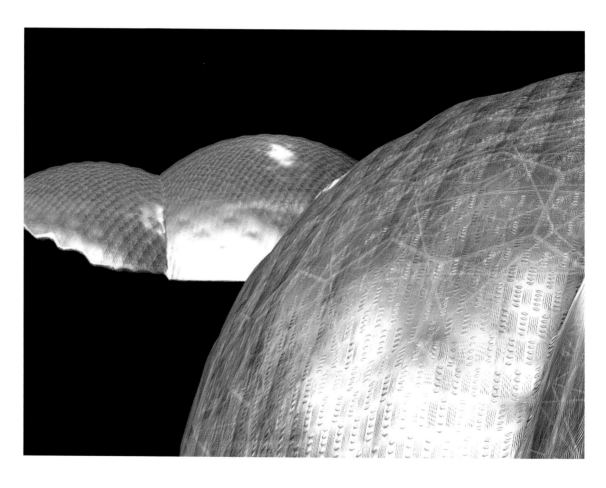

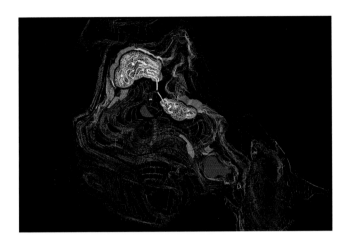

**Nicholas Grimshaw & Partners: Eden Project
Visitor Centre, Cornwall**
The color-coded plans create intricate abstract patterns.

The Eden Project is intended to be a participatory polemic for global bio-diversity, demonstrating our dependence on plants. A series of interlocking, climate-controlled "biomes," closely integrated into a 5 1/2-acre (2.2-hectare) site, open up to visitors after they enter through an information center where micro and time lapse photography describe the plant types they will see. The biomes, enclosed by an "exoskeleton" of lightweight steel wrapped in a soft clear membrane, are divided into humid, tropic, and warm temperate regions, with emphasis placed on the contrast between inside and outside through the treatment of the exterior landscape near the biomes. Spherical geometry provided the strongest, lightest structure – of minimal surface and maximum volume – built of straight tubular compressive members joined by standard cast connections, which are configured in a hexagonal cell geometry with a 30-foot (9-meter) span. The hexagons are clad with transparent, inflated "pillows" that combine to make an extremely light envelope.

The biomes, designed to be additive, will have different diameters depending on spatial requirements, intentionally giving the impression of a biomorphic organism – the paradox of computer generation used to reproduce natural forms once again, but at a much less fundamental level than the work of John Frazer or Karl Chu.

From Biosphere to Stratosphere

Grimshaw & Partners also chose spherical geometry for the National Space Science Centre, an educational and research facility linked to the University of Leicester, England, in a pivotal position between the historic Abbey Pumping Station and Riverside Park. The Centre's main exhibition space occupies converted underground storm water tanks – which have been roofed over – and the dome that penetrates this new roof plane mirrors the form of a planetarium that is also part of the new facility. The dome is treated as the center of a nebular vortex, generating a spiraling geometry that spins upward from the entrance courtyard, around a ramp and into the surrounding landscape, tying the Centre to its context. The idea of relative perception, which is crucial to an understanding of space and space research, is partially conveyed by the orientation and vertical

Nicholas Grimshaw & Partners: NSSC, Leicester
The new National Space Science Centre occupies a
strategic position in the town between the Abbey Pumping
Station and Riverside Park.

Nicholas Grimshaw & Partners: NSSC, Leicester
Roofed-over storm water tanks are penetrated by a glass
enclosed tower that announces the planetarium.

angle walls in the exhibition hall. The depth and construction
method used on these walls allowed for the integration of a large-
scale public artwork which uses light and anamorphic projection to
challenge conventional notions of depth perception, while a tower
that marks the end of the exhibition sequence symbolizes the
different technologies that will play a role in future space
exploration and development. A minimal steel structure supports
a three-layer skin of patterned ETFE foil that is pneumatically
inflated to form lightweight pillows.

In Sybaritic Hot Water, Inspired by Decimus Burton

The computer also helped the Grimshaw & Partners decipher the
complex geometry used to solve the problem of how to integrate
a new spa into six existing buildings, three of which are listed, in
the historic Georgian city of Bath in southwest England. Located
in the Cross and Healing Springs area at the western end of Bath
Street, which has a long association with spa bathing, the project
is intended to revitalize the only natural hot springs in the United
Kingdom – unused since 1978 – for both medical and leisure
purposes. The local council has teamed up with a Dutch spa
operator, Thermae Developments, to join together the buildings
at 7–7a and 8 Bath Street, the hot bath itself, and an open site
where the Beau Street building once stood into a combination
of new and refurbished buildings that will attract people to Bath
to "take the waters" once again.

In such sensitive circumstances in this World Heritage site,
the conceptual attitude that was taken up is similar to the
archaeological principle adopted as part of the Venice Charter –
of making new additions to the existing fabric clearly legible, by
materials and articulation, so as not to pass off new for old. The
site of the demolished Beau Street building will be occupied by

what will be the only new building in the complex: a three-story,
free-standing cube of golden Bath stone, proportioned to relate to
the Hot Baths adjacent to it. Large-scale columns supporting the
top of the cube emerge from a free-form pool that acts as a foil to
this geometry. This cube will be pierced with glass lenses, which
will diffuse natural daylight as it filters down through the steam
rising from the pool, similar to the *omriyyad* of a traditional Turkish
bath. Four free-standing, circular, glass-enclosed steam rooms will
be located under each of the conical column capitals.

The space around these steam rooms will have wide benches
for resting, while a central oculus will direct light through a cold
mist spray. Elevators, as well as a helical stair and subsidiary stairs,
will lead to a multi-leveled rooftop terrace, which will provide views
down to the main pool from varying heights, as well as of the
other baths and the nearby hills that surround the city.

One would hardly suspect that all of this quasi-Roman sybaritic
splendor occurs behind a delicately detailed rational glass façade,
carefully configured to follow the sinuous street line. The
relationship between this non-rectilinear glazed boundary wall and
the strict geometry of the cube it contains deliberately recalls the
curved screen walls that the nineteenth-century builder Decimus
Burton used to enclose the Hot Baths, designed in the Palladian
style by John Woods the Younger, confirming the connection
between the current leaders of the high-tech spirit in Britain and
the best practitioners of steel and glass conservatory engineering
during the Industrial Revolution.

Nicholas Grimshaw & Partners:
Bath Street development, Bath
The new spa is located at the western end of Bath Street,
in the Cross and Healing Springs area.

Nicholas Grimshaw & Partners:
Bath Street development, Bath
Few existing urban conditions are as delicate as the Georgian
city of Bath, and Grimshaw Partnership has provided a new
facility with great sensitivity.

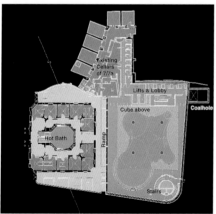

Nicholas Grimshaw & Partners:
Bath Street development, Bath
The heart of the new spa is a three-story cube
clad in Bath stone, pierced with glass lenses that
strategically direct light into the interior.

Cesar Pelli: Petronas Towers, Kuala Lumpur
The skybridge that links the towers at midpoint was lowered into place by helicopters, while millions of Malaysians watched on television.

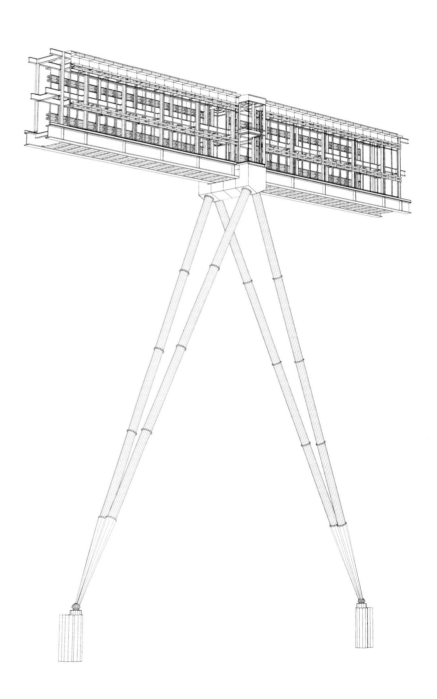

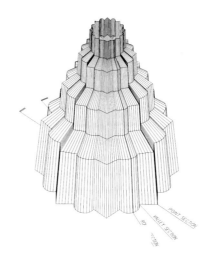

Cesar Pelli: Petronas Towers, Kuala Lumpur
Computer graphics have made it possible to reinterpret traditional Islamic patterns in the form of the Twin Towers.

Twin Beacons of a Super Media Society

Cesar Pelli is frequently mentioned in the same breath as high-tech and his stunning design for the Petronas Towers (1996) in Kuala Lumpur, Malaysia, also fits Foster's Swiss Re model of using computer assistance to describe extremely complex forms, which in turn changes the image of the high-rise. In Malaysia the geometrical component was even more of an essential ingredient of the concept, given the delicate social balance there between the predominantly Islamic, indigenous Malays, and the Chinese and Indian minorities, which differentiates the nation from any other country in Asia. The brief distributed to those invited to participate in the international competition for Phase One of the Kuala Lumpur City Center directed that the architecture should be "Malaysian", and Pelli was told, after winning, that he was the only one to address this requirement. In his rationale for the project, he describes how he

> tried to relate to the climate, to the dominant Islamic culture, and to the sense of form and patterning that I could perceive in traditional Malaysian buildings and objects (and) to avoid any sense of a culture pastiche… The geometry of the towers is based on Islamic geometric traditions. These geometric traditions are much more important in Islamic countries than in the West and are understood, perceived and appreciated by everyone in their society. The plan of the building is based on the geometry of two interlocked squares, which is perhaps the most important geometric form underlying Islamic designs. The interlocking squares create an 8-pointed star. To this form we superimposed 8 semi-circles in the inner angles of the star creating a 16-branched form. In each of the 16 inner angles we have smaller semi-circular forms expressing the main structural columns of the building. The development of the geometry from simple to complex forms also follows Islamic tradition. The basic square represents the earth and its four

cardinal points (or heaven and its four rivers) and complexity is a necessary development to reflect the incomprehensibility of God. Each tower as it ascends sets back six times, and in the upper set backs the walls tilt gently toward the center, complementing the form and strengthening the axis mundi of the skyscraper. The top spires reach to the sky and reinforce the representative quality of the silhouette.

Along with the strategy of using geometry to socially contextualize the towers, Pelli feels that a decision of parallel importance was the choice of a "figurative and symmetrical composition" which focuses attention on the void between the towers, rather than the asymmetrical groupings of pairs favored by the modern movement. He believes that "the symmetrical arrangement was avoided by early modernists precisely because of its symbolic quality. The towers we designed are not only symmetrical but figurative, creating an also figurative space between them. This space is the key element in the composition. Each tower has its own vertical axis, but the axis of the total composition is in the center of the void. Lao Tse has taught us that the reality of a hollow object is in the void and not in the walls that define it."

Pelli took advantage of this central focus by placing a pedestrian bridge between the two towers, to create a sky lobby between the forty-first and forty-second floors, 560 feet (170 meters) above the ground – "a portal to the sky" and "door to the infinite." The skybridge, which spans 192 feet (58.44 meters) and weighs over 720 tons, was prefabricated on the ground and lifted into place in an engineering feat that captivated the Malaysian public when broadcast live on television. There was a collective sigh of relief when the 169-foot- (51.5-meter-) long diagonal struts finally swung into place; the precision of this achievement is second only to the brief reign of the towers as the tallest skyscraper in the world as a source of national pride.

Cesar Pelli: Petronas Towers, Kuala Lumpur
The real significance of the Twin Towers is that it reconciles conflicting Asian and Western ideologies.

The 451.9-meter- (1,482-foot-) high, 88-story towers are clad in stainless steel spandrel panels interspersed with horizonal ribbons of vision glass. These are particularly suited to the volatile Malaysian climate, reflecting the sudden changes in the color of the sky when sunny haze is replaced by the black storm clouds that seem to roll in at one time or another each day, or by the spectacular palettes of sunset. They are also effectively lit at night, seeming to sparkle in the darkness, offering a constant point of reference visible from every part of the city.

Virtual Recovery of a Lost Heritage
In his design for the King Saud Mosque in the Kingdom of Saudi Arabia, London-based architect Abdel Wahed El-Wakil also relied entirely on computer technology to replicate the *muqarnas* or stalactite mouldings carved above the main entrance of the Sultan Hasan Mosque in Cairo. The use of geometry for El-Wakil represents far more than a means of conveying an Islamic character, it is symbolic of repairing a link in a chain of convention extending back to the beginning of the faith, broken in the rejection of craft that followed the Industrial Revolution, and manifested in the disappearance of ornamental detail. First trying conventional representation in his attempt to uncover the lost secrets of geometric detail in *muqarnas* construction, El-Wakil soon realized that the patterns and theorems that generated them were too complex. He then bought every computer manual he could find in the late 1980s to help him in his self-taught search. Whenever he hears about a building of Fatimid or Mamluk vintage that has either collapsed or is being demolished in the medieval quarter of Cairo – which happens far too frequently – he tries to get there before the pieces are carted off in order to record the way they fit together. This record is now made with a digital camera. He always finds surprises in the way the parts interlock; each one is like a new jigsaw puzzle waiting to be solved.

The King Saud Mosque entrance, which is an exact replica of the Sultan Hasan doorway, caused a great deal of controversy when it first appeared, and the debate about the issues it raises still continues. Detractors condemn it as a blatant copy that has no relevance in its new setting, while El-Wakil and his defenders believe that originality is a modernist conceit. They argue that insistence on singularity is arrogant, and irrelevant in traditional representation, in which a design evolves from and relies upon precedents. In El-Wakil's opinion, replication is a necessary, unavoidable first step on the convoluted pathway back to where the rupture between craft and mechanized product occurred, and this point must be reached before typologically based invention can begin again. El-Wakil chooses to use mechanization to return to the point before it destroyed the craft he is trying to reconstruct, and he was one of the first among a growing number of architects trying to protect their heritage against the depredations of globalization to do so.

Abdel Wahed El-Wakil: King Saud Mosque, Saudi Arabia
As globalization spreads, many cultures have intensified the search for authenticity.

Abdel Wahed El-Wakil: King Saud Mosque, Saudi Arabia
The *muqarnas* of the Sultan Hasan Mosque in Cairo served as the model for the doorway of the King Saud Mosque.

**Arata Isozaki: Center of Science and Industry,
Columbus, Ohio**
Some architects have used the computer as a means of
refining formal purity.

**Arata Isozaki: Center of Science and Industry,
Columbus, Ohio**
A cylindrical form breaks through the curved shell of the
Science Center to announce the entrance.

Kisho Kurokawa: Van Gogh Museum, Amsterdam
Bold geometries allow the Van Gogh Museum to achieve its own
identity while still respecting its famous neighbors.

Kisho Kurokawa: Van Gogh Museum, Amsterdam
A lower-level entry provides a more secluded feeling, in contrast to the
frenetic activity on the Museumplein above.

Intricacy Versus Simplicity

As Kisho Kurokawa's new Van Gogh Museum (1996) in
Amsterdam demonstrates, not all computer applications – among
those who use them as a tool to enhance personal expression –
relate to solving previously impenetrable geometric configurations.
Kurokawa has used the computer as an editing device instead,
in his own progression toward even more potent and memorable
forms. His point is that the information age has decreased mental
and visual attention spans, and in the frenetically fast-paced
competition to implant a durable image, less is definitely more.

As an addition to the big three on the Museumplein in
Amsterdam – the Cuypers Rijksmuseum, the Stedelijk Museum
of Modern Art, and the existing Van Gogh Museum, posthumously
reconstructed in 1973 from an original design by Gerrit Rietveld –
the Kurokawa extension strikes a delicate balance between
respectfulness and being feisty, with its metaphorical cocked hat
and unmistakable individuality. Kurokawa's enduring themes of
metabolism (mutation) and symbiosis (living together), which are
increasingly appropriate as globalism expands, surface here in a
sunken semi-elliptical plaza that mediates between De Stijl and
the future. The plaza opens out from the single below-grade level
of Kurokawa's addition, which leans in deferential friendship
toward its predecessor. A boxy, subtly gridded projection, pushing
out from this canted wall, seems as if it is extended out toward the
similar modular forms of the Rietveld original. The complexity here,
then, is bound up in intention rather than in the presentation of
intentional formal complexity as a recital of cybernetic virtuosity,
and as such is a laudable exercise in restraint.

A similar strategy of discipline masking complex intention is
evident on a much larger scale at the Center of Science and
Industry (1999) in Columbus, Ohio, by Arata Isozaki. Isozaki
shared with Kurokawa a mentor – Kenzo Tange – as well as a
brief commitment to Metabolism, and they are both now among
the leaders of the generation of Japanese architects who matured
and prospered during the post-war economic boom. They now
also seem to share a desire to simplify their forms. The Center
of Science and Industry, or COSI, replaces a 30-year-old facility
near the Scioto River in Columbus, and uses part of a 1920s
high school to anchor the center of an elongated, boat-shaped
museum. The 320,000-square-foot (29,450-square-meter),
monumental ark is organized along a 960-foot (293-meter)
central circulation spine, and is sheathed by 50-by-10-foot
(15-by-3-meter) light gray precast panels that provide a protective
carapace for the fantasy world inside. The massiveness of the
panels, which marks a new level of monumentality for Isozaki,
is only relieved by stainless steel joints that have a surprising
amount of reflectivity. The seven self-contained "learning worlds"
distributed along the central spine, along with two theaters and
a skylit atrium, conform to the emphasis on interactive exhibits
that is prevalent in most new museums, with computers much
in evidence.

Coop Himmelb(l)au: UFA Cinema, Dresden
The collision of the cinema block and the Crystal entry hall has resulted in a vertical circulation vortex, sheathed in glass.

Coop Himmelb(l)au: UFA Cinema, Dresden
Aggressive forms have been tactically employed to break down the monolithic character of public space.

Coop Himmelb(l)au: SEG Tower, Vienna
The SEG Tower is one of the largest urban projects by Coop Himmelb(l)au to date.

Coop Himmelb(l)au Protects Public Space

The restraint shown in the Amsterdam and Columbus museums is nowhere in evidence in Dresden, where the battle lines over the future of public space in this and other large European cities are more clearly drawn. The UFA Cinema Center by Coop Himmelb(l)au, designed and built between 1993 and 1998, is a deliberately assertive strategy to "disintegrate" the single-function monoliths now filling the precious, rapidly diminishing number of public spaces that financially insolvent city governments are forced to sell to developers. As part of a broadbased urban concept developed for the Tragerstrasse Nord competition, defined by dynamic spatial sequences organized along tangents and diagonals instead of a single axis, the UFA Cinema Center is at a junction of an interweaving of public squares, public interiors, and passageways that the architects hope will "energize and densify" the new center of Dresden, providing a model for other cities to follow.

The UFA complex is made up of two intricately interconnected units – the Cinema Block and the Crystal – conceived as a bi-polar junction between the Pragerplatz and St. Petersburger Strasse. The Cinema Block opens up to the street and is "permeable" to people walking between Pragerstrasse and St. Petersburger Strasse; the circulation system leading to each of the cinemas in the block has intentionally been designed to activate this junction and entice people inside. The Crystal has been conceived not merely as a functional entry hall for the cinemas, but as an "urban passageway" into what the architects view as an "inside-out" building whose contents are entirely visible to the city. Its bridges, ramps, and stairs are "urban expressions" purposefully angled to maximize people-watching from a number of levels.

Coop Himmelb(l)au: SEG Tower, Vienna
Graphics can now capture the mood that the
architects intend a space to have.

From City Center to New Center

The SEG apartment tower in Vienna was opened in 1998 in a new district called Donau-City, between Wagramerstrasse and Kratachwilestrasse and adjacent to the Alte Donau metro station. It is the first of three such high-rises to be built there, marking an attempt to distribute the public focus on the city center to other zones. The mixed-use tower has 70 apartments, as well as offices and restaurants, on 25 floors and has been positioned to take advantage of its proximity to one of the most popular recreational districts in Vienna. Each of the two distinct office and residential areas in the tower has been treated as being accommodated in a "house." The "houses," when stacked on top of each other, are intersected with a sky lobby which contains a cybercafé and playground.

Marking a novel change of direction for the firm, the tower has a "smart" glass sheath uniting the two stacked houses, which works in conjunction with an "air box" on the roof to regulate the summer and winter temperatures that can be surprisingly extreme in Vienna. This "climate façade," which appears uniform on the outside, masks unexpectedly dynamic loft-like apartment sections. These glazed façades, which protect two- and three-story-high planted conservatories, literally make this a green building.

The decision by Coop Himmelb(l)au to replicate the media – by patterning the circulation sequence at UFA on that of a film, and by making the synapse of SEG a cybercafé – shows how endemic the electronic culture has become. The computer has not only been used as a tool to create these complex shapes, but also as an integral symbol of the revised cultural purpose of each project, which is consistent with each of the other examples included here.

chapter 2
adapting catia

120

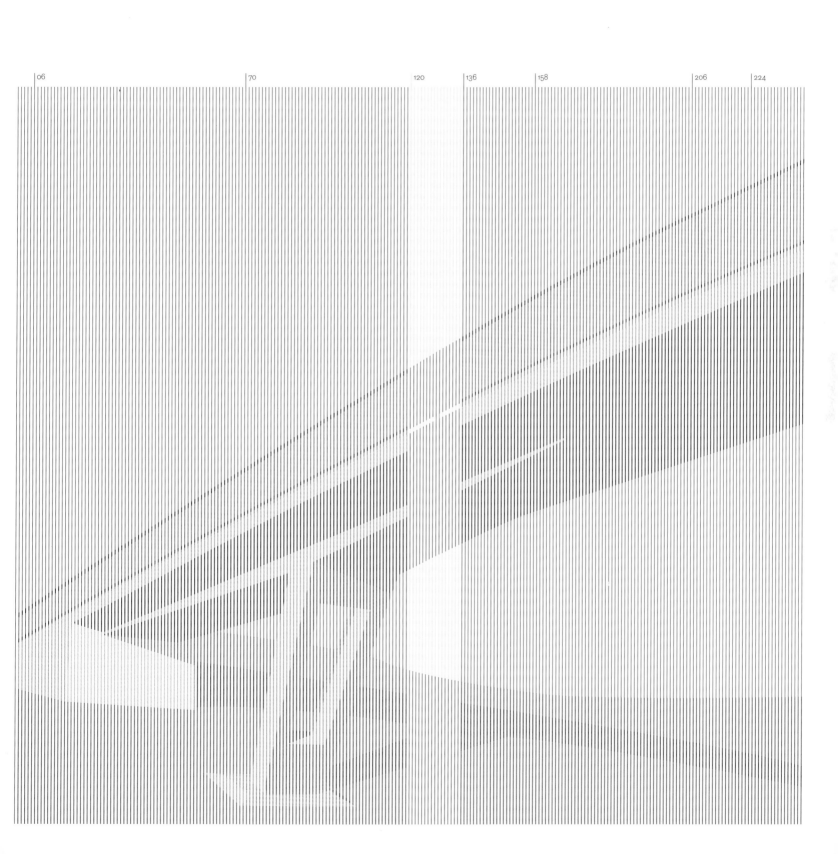

ADAPTING CATIA

Frank Gehry, whose specialized adaptation of the CATIA mechanical design system has revolutionized what had primarily been an engineering application, insists that he doesn't use it as a design tool. Believing instead that "the imagery on the computer takes the juice out of an idea," he emphatically claims: "I can't stand it!" First developed in the Gehry office in 1989 during the design of a large sculpture for the Olympic Village in Barcelona, the specific techniques that eventually made the Guggenheim Bilbao possible have been adapted from the CATIA Program. While the program was initially introduced into the office for the Barcelona project, the challenges faced in the Los Angeles Disney Concert Hall design – the unconventional configuration of the proposed hall defied traditional methods of documentation – also played a key role in pushing the historic transfer of this technology from aeronautical engineering to architecture. The competition-winning scheme for the proposed new cultural locus of Grand Avenue had been based on a fan-shaped seating arrangement that the architect felt had formal possibilities, but after Gehry received the commission, a subsequent consultation with a new acoustician radically changed the design direction. This advice dictated that the fan be changed to a shoebox-shaped hall, leading Gehry to design a curvaceous wrapper to soften the severe lines of the rectilinear core. Gehry's long-term interest in art, his self-image as an artist-architect,

and his particular knowledge of Russian Constructivism – a movement that advocated a complete rethinking of the ways in which function influences form – emerges most clearly in his stream-of-consciousness sketching technique. It can also be seen in his hands-on use of innumerable scale models, which he constantly rips apart and alters by cutting and pasting new layers on top of old. This collage technique, which was also favoured by Constructivist artists during the 1920s, resulted in many curvilinear surfaces. These curves, applied over the Concert Hall core, could only be converted from model to preliminary documents by painstaking methods of graphic projection that have remained essentially unchanged since the Renaissance. Gehry's self-imposed deadline for exhibiting the design at the Venice Biennale, which included a full-scale mock-up of a portion of the exterior wall of the Concert Hall – then conceived as limestone mounted on a hidden steel structural frame – brought on a production mini-crisis, forcing the issue of how to accurately represent the architect's models in a larger-scale building. CATIA saved the day, allowing a segment of the wall to be constructed in Venice on time. Activated by a hand-held probe which transfers the complex curves of a scale model to a computer screen when it is run across each significant slope, CATIA not only made precise documentation possible, but also allowed details to be conveyed to a stonecutter on a diskette that guided the blades directly.

Frank Gehry: Disney Concert Hall
An acoustician's recommendation for a rectilinear hall led
Gehry to use a wrapper that offset its straight lines.

Frank Gehry: Disney Concert Hall
The way the concert hall looked before its redesign,
with stone rather than its new metal sheathing.

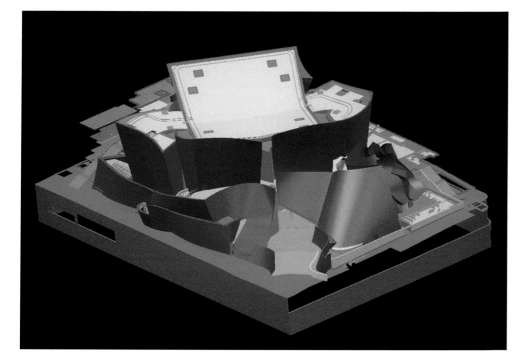

Frank Gehry: Disney Concert Hall
As studies evolve, they take on a life of their own.

Frank Gehry: Disney Concert Hall
The juxtaposition of the space enclosure and the wrapper revealed key points of divergence.

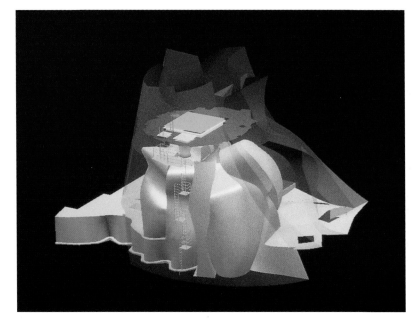

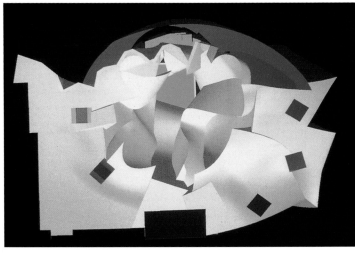

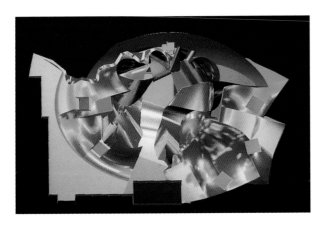

Frank Gehry: Disney Concert Hall
The color coding of various elements created an
expressionistic diagram.

A Brief History of CATIA

In 1976 IBM launched its 2250 Graphics Display System, one of
the first terminals to support CAD vector-based graphics, which
could be attached to general purpose mainframes and was mainly
used to support specific applications. Then in 1982 the company
announced the first version of the CATIA mechanical design
system. CATIA was developed by Dassault Systèmes, a subsidiary
of the French aircraft manufacturer of Mirage jet fighters, in order
to add surface modeling and numerical control capabilities to
an existing design system. Since then, however, CATIA has been
continuously used to support the entire design process, from
conceptualization through manufacturing, in a non-proprietary way
that allows data interchange. CATIA's workhorse capacity has
been demonstrated by its developers' continued dependence on
it. Dassault Aviation also relied on CATIA for the design and
production of the Rafale jet fighter and the Falcon jet. [67]

Difficulties with Disney

The euphoria over having solved the problem of how to represent
and document such difficult curves on the Disney Concert Hall,
which radically altered Gehry's design direction in such a relatively
short period of time, was short-lived, however, as costs spiraled
upward due to factors beyond the architect's control and beyond
the scope of this discussion. Embittered by the misunderstandings
that began to deconstruct what may now be historically seen
as his breakthrough project in form, function, and scale, Gehry
railed against his misinformed critics, published apologia in the
press, and turned his back on the city with which he had become
so closely associated as architectural therapist and alter ego.

The discovery of CATIA's capability led next to the Frederick R.
Weisman Art and Teaching Museum (1992) at the University of
Minnesota in Minneapolis, a clear and conscious expression of
creative ideas in transition en route to the final realization at
Bilbao. Located on a tightly constricted campus site that was
bounded by a bridge, a plaza, a street, and an academic building,
the museum seems to burst down a slope and reach out toward
the Mississippi and the view of the Minneapolis skyline across
it in a Cubist symphony of metallic forms that has been likened
to Marcel Duchamp's *Nude Descending a Staircase*. In a move
that underscores the architect's inherent pragmatism — and
undoubtedly pleases the museum administrators who are typically
stuck away in basement offices, but here get pride of place with
high views overlooking the river — Gehry has placed the galleries
in a rectilinear configuration extending back from the exuberant
Cubist face, which presents a more sedate brick façade to the
neighborhood. The building achieves a seemingly unlikely, but
carefully implemented balance between meeting the demands
of a good academic citizen and presenting a memorable public
face that is now the requisite of all contemporary museums.
The rectilinear galleries, which are accessed by bridge from the
campus plaza, fit in well with their surroundings, while the
sandblasted, stainless steel assemblage facing the city echoes
the flow of the river and presents a shining visage to the public.
As Coop Himmelb(l)au's Wolf Prix said, while serving as a
member of a jury that cited the building for excellence when
it opened in 1992: "It's beautiful to see how a loft mutates into
a mask."

Coop Himmelb(l)au, along with Arata Isozaki and Frank Gehry,
was also shortlisted as a possible architect for a new museum
for Bilbao, Spain, being considered by Thomas Krens, director of
the Guggenheim Museum in New York. Krens' eventual choice
of Gehry led to the creation of a building that, due to a special
set of circumstances, became one of the architectural milestones
of the twentieth century. [68]

Frank Gehry: Frederick R. Weisman Art Museum, Minneapolis
The river façade of the Weisman Museum is clearly a precursor of the Bilbao Guggenheim.

Frank Gehry: Guggenheim, Bilbao
The metallic shell of Gehry's tour de force blends into the industrial district around it.

The Bilbao Museum as Contemporary Cathedral

The first of these circumstances is the radical change that has taken place in the museum as public institution recently. Having begun in the late seventeenth and early eighteenth centuries as mere cabinets or roomsful of curiosities in houses of the rich, the museum eventually evolved into a freestanding venue in which both artifacts and art could be viewed by the general public as a means of educating and elevating popular taste. It has now, however, been transformed into a destination in its own right. In response to radical social changes that have occurred over the last four decades, boards of directors and curators have attempted to make museums more responsive to public desires. They have been attempting to change their reputation for being stuffy, hidebound, self-righteous enclaves of aesthetic and sociological artifacts; or time capsules preserving the best of civilization for only the deserving few who were willing to pay the price of admission and undergo the physical demands of marching along seemingly endless corridors.

With the advent of globalization, however, which may also be characterized as final proof of the prevalence and internationalization of popular Western – and specifically American – culture, museum boards have seen the handwriting, if not the graffiti, on the wall. They have become committed to making this venerable institution more accessible. Paradoxically, the same social transformations that have prompted this new transparency have also induced a retrograde attitude about museums, especially among urban administrators and city planners, causing them now to be seen as the last bastions of good taste, or as the sacred repositories of the highest and best that the curators themselves no longer want them to be. This curiously nostalgic perception, undoubtedly resulting from the seemingly unstoppable proliferation of homogeneity, has made a new museum, along with a theater (which has also come to represent "culture"), a must in any city that now wants to be taken seriously.

Bilbao, which is perfectly pleasant but certainly not known as a must-see hot spot among the burgeoning number of world travelers, is one of these cities. Once ranking well below the soporific delights of Patagonia among most travelers, Bilbao was a well kept secret among aficionados who valued it for its orderly formality and cleanliness, overlaying Basque pride, volubility, and eccentricity. Because of the Guggenheim, Bilbao has now been elevated almost instantaneously into a point of pilgrimage as a cultural capital. Much as Santiago de Compostela, which is further along the same coastline, was for religious devotees during the Middle Ages, the Guggenheim Museum in Bilbao seems to cause rapture among those who eventually reach it. It is the equivalent of a cathedral in the digital age, filling the void left by a general decline in religious faith, but the relics here – the art on the walls and floor – are not venerated nearly as much as the museum itself. This is one of the most obvious cases of the phenomenon that has accompanied the contemporary elevation of the museum to the position of a symbol of high culture in an age of deteriorating taste: the art inside is redundant.

An important difference between Romanesque pilgrimage churches or Gothic cathedrals and the Bilbao museum – the second significant circumstance that influenced the museum's design – is that of the new materials and technology available to the architect today. After a painstaking search, Gehry chose titanium rather than troublesome limestone as a skin, because he liked the way it seems to shimmer in the light reflecting off the river right next to it, subtly echoing but certainly not replicating the metallic edge of the industries nearby.

Frank Gehry: Guggenheim, Bilbao
The nexus of the Bilbao Guggenheim is the
contemporary version of the nave of a Gothic cathedral.

The building is a thoroughbred deliberately let loose among dray horses; they are the same species but the similarity stops there. The cathedral analogy is appropriate because no other historical comparison seems to apply; the builders of Reims or Chartres sought to use the highest engineering skills and best materials available to them to reproduce the heavenly Jerusalem on earth for the glory of God, as described by John the Evangelist in the Book of Revelations. In this increasingly secular age CATIA has now allowed the architect to achieve tectonic contortions that no Gothic mason could ever imagine, let alone replicate. Philip Johnson loves the Bilbao Guggenheim, calling it the most important building of our time. He said that he wept when he saw the interior of the museum, presumably because it provides irrefutable proof that the electronic revolution has finally, definitively supplanted its industrial predecessor, and that his profession will never face the same repressive physical restrictions again.

Separatist Symbol
The third facet of the significance of the Bilbao museum, which complicates matters even further, is the ongoing debate over its possible role as a symbol of the Basque desire to separate from Spain. The Basques argue that they have a completely different history, language and tradition than the rest of the country, and feel their spiritual capital is in Bilbao. They have pursued independence for decades, and their determination to have an American with a firmly established international reputation as the architect of this showpiece institution has been interpreted by some as being part of that agenda. A counter argument is that the choice of Gehry represents nothing more than an attempt by a city that is comfortably prosperous, but was certainly not well known, to elevate itself to world class status. Based on the millions of tourists that now travel to Bilbao each year specifically

to visit the museum, which opened in 1997, the city has arguably succeeded in that goal. Because it effectively combines these three complex strands – cutting edge technology that has made previously undreamt of spaces possible; the changing, paradoxically double-coded new role of the museum; and the separatist frisson that seems to be sweeping around the world to counter the homogeneity of globalization – the Bilbao Guggenheim is indeed a fitting symbol of the technological changes that make the move into a new century.

**Gehry's Importance in the
Computer Revolution in Architecture**
The importance of CATIA's coming of age in the hands of Gehry and his design and production team at Bilbao goes beyond its providing the ability to manipulate and document the complicated shapes that the architect first sketches and models, by allowing the architect to finally build them. There was a tight $100 million budget for the Guggenheim which the city could not exceed, and CATIA is credited with helping deliver the building within that cost by saving time and ensuring the efficient application of materials. The firm's principal Jim Glymph recalls CATIA first being introduced to solve the structural complexities of a large fish sculpture that Gehry designed for the Villa Olympica in Barcelona between 1989 and 1992. Glymph maintains that what sets CATIA apart from other systems is its use of polynomial equations, so that instead of simply locating points in space, as other systems do, CATIA is also "capable of defining any surface as an equation, which means that if you query the computer for any point on that surface, it knows it." This high degree of accuracy was augmented by the design team, who customized it to suit their own approach. Glymph describes this personalization as "a process through digitizing and visualization on the screen… where we started to capture the physical mode. And unlike

Frank Gehry: Guggenheim, Bilbao
Like its counterpart in New York, the Bilbao Guggenheim
reinterprets its setting.

everybody else, we always went back to the physical model." [69]
Gehry was skeptical at first, but once he recognized the ability
of CATIA to translate his graphic and cardboard collage design
gestures and its capacity to document complicated shapes in a
way that did not baffle or intimidate contractors, he became a
convert. The knowledge that he need no longer restrain his
imagination to insure buildability was liberating for Gehry, as
the exuberance of the Guggenheim Bilbao demonstrates. [70]

Rather than distancing the architect even further from the
construction process, then, as some believe the abstract exercise
of computing has the potential to do, Gehry believes it will finally
earn the profession more respect from contractors and clients
because of the accuracy in documentation, budgeting, bidding,
and manufacturing that it makes possible. Whether or not this
degree of accuracy is only possible using the ad hoc system
he has developed is an open question that invites further
investigation. With his stunning success in Bilbao, which has led
to a flood of new commissions throughout the world, Gehry is
now poised to eclipse Frank Lloyd Wright, his early hero, as the
greatest American architect. He has now even received the
ultimate accolade of being featured along with the likes of Maria
Callas and Miles Davis on Mackintosh's multistory "Think
Different" billboards throughout Los Angeles, which is ironic,
considering how Gehry has been treated there.

Now that the Disney Concert Hall is back on track, with a
new metallic skin, it is possible that the architect once generally
acknowledged to be the most insightful translator of the
complicated soul of the centerless city of Los Angeles may
actually return to this role. Gehry was, at one time, referred to
as the leader of the "Los Angeles School," a group of younger
architects that included Frank Israel, Morphosis, and Eric Owen
Moss, whose rapidly proliferating list of built anomalies in Culver
City continues to receive disbelieving media attention. But
promising talent Frank Israel is now tragically deceased,
Morphosis has bifurcated, and Moss has decried what he
divisively refers to as the "Snow White and Seven Dwarves"
theory of the contemporary architectural scene in Los Angeles.
All of this is taking place amidst speculation that the center of
the avant-garde has shifted to London and Rotterdam, and that
the Los Angeles School, if there ever was such a group, was an
Eighties thing, well matched with the wretched excess that the
decade was best known for. Minimalism is in fashion now – less
is more again, more or less – and Frank Gehry cannot come
home again, in the stylistic sense, especially in the light of the
worldwide status he has acquired as a result of the Bilbao
Guggenheim. CATIA has certainly opened up a new creative door,
but many wonder where this technology will lead, and if it has a
threshold, since it is pure form without a solid theoretical basis.
For Gehry, the real miracle of this breakthrough is that he has
been able to sustain formal momentum and variety after Bilbao.

Frank Gehry: Guggenheim, Bilbao
Gehry has led a quiet revolution by pioneering CATIA
in architecture.

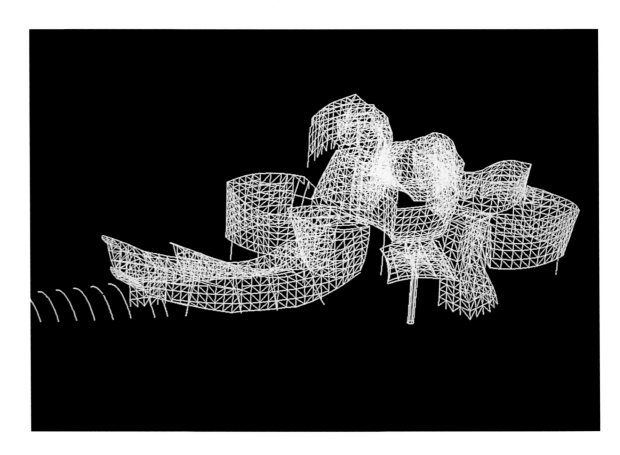

Gehry Redefines Modernity

The recent resurgence of modernism, after more than three decades of disfavor, has once again brought such questions about the nature of a true versus a superficial style to the forefront of discussions about the future of architecture. Theorists, philosophers, and historians continue to debate the many meanings of modernity and modernism; the consensus is that modernity is a state of being, while modernism is, in architectural terms, a style. As a style that began to eclipse traditionalism soon after the beginning of the twentieth century, the proponents of which advocated the use of newly available industrial materials and scientific advances in the formation of stripped-down buildings with no legible historical reference, modernism seemed to have run its course by the mid-1960s. Failed attempts to reintroduce traditional and historical elements back into buildings, however, as well as public disenchantment with the misguided efforts of historicists to interpret cultural symbols have now prompted a resurgence of the modern style. This may also be ascribed to a collective nostalgia for a time when the idea of progress was unassailable, things seemed more predictable, and the future looked unquestionably secure.

Frank Gehry's approach, as demonstrated in Bilbao, is far from modernism as a style and yet is the essence of what it means to be modern. The result of a specialized kind of computer technology, which that architect is responsible for introducing to the profession, and boasting an exterior cladding which is equally novel, this Guggenheim is as ahead of its time as Frank Lloyd Wright's shocking concrete spiral was when the Guggenheim opened in New York City in the late 1950s. An embodiment of the phrase "pushing the envelope," the Bilbao Guggenheim may now have initiated a style of its own. Copycat structures by other designers have begun to spring up like mushrooms in cities all over the world. If imitation really is the sincerest form of flattery, these clones may be the highest of all tributes to the real significance of Gehry's breakthrough.

Factory Futures

The accuracy in documentation and manufacture that CATIA makes possible is borne out in the extensive use of that system for engineering projects. One such example is the Chrysler Corporation Assembly Plant in Toledo, Ohio, designed by Joel Rosenbaum, CADD Coordinator at BEI Associates in Detroit, one of the largest architectural engineering firms in Michigan. The three main automobile manufacturers in Detroit spend over $7 billion on new construction each year, and when Daimler Chrysler decided to build a $1.2 billion plant in Toledo – the first auto plant to open in the United States in 2000 – the company decided to make it also the first to be designed using three-dimensional computer graphics, to save time and money. They estimate that this decision allowed them to reduce the usual design and construction schedule by six months. CATIA allowed the designer to verify the need for each length of wire, duct, or steel beam. This visualization led to such improvements as a more accurate roof configuration on which air conditioning units and other equipment could be located only where needed to reduce steel sections, and a system whereby electric power is delivered by a central spine that can be extended as needed in the future, rather than through a uniform overhead grid. A three-dimensional animated fly-through of the various departments in the factory allowed plant engineers to eliminate possible obstacles in the production line, and they estimate that over 300 potential obstructions – which otherwise would have been missed – were avoided using digital mapping, amounting to a savings of about half a million dollars.[71]

This plant was a pilot project for a larger strategy by Daimler Chrysler – called the Digital Model Assembly Process System – to integrate all products on a totally integrated CATIA platform. Rosenbaum recalls a change in attitude about CATIA soon after design started. He and his team, who were used to 3D micro stations, said they soon realized they were dealing with an "intelligent" system, which can be accessed, as long as the building lasts, for needs and replacement strategies.

BEI Associates: Chrysler Plant, Toledo, Ohio
Engineers have also found CATIA to be an invaluable tool in
sorting out interlocking elements.

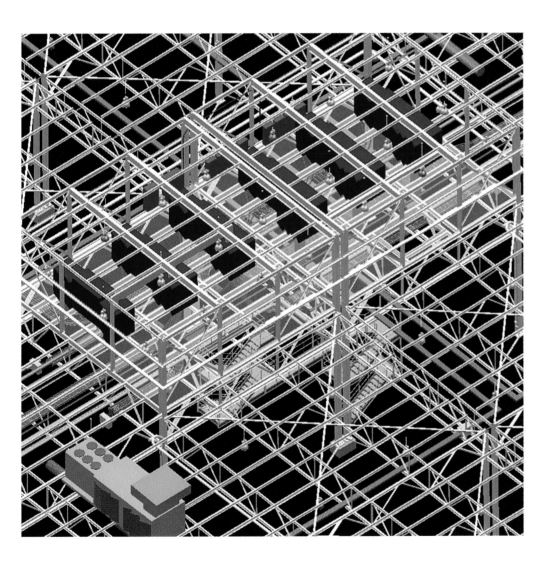

chapter 3
letting the computer lead

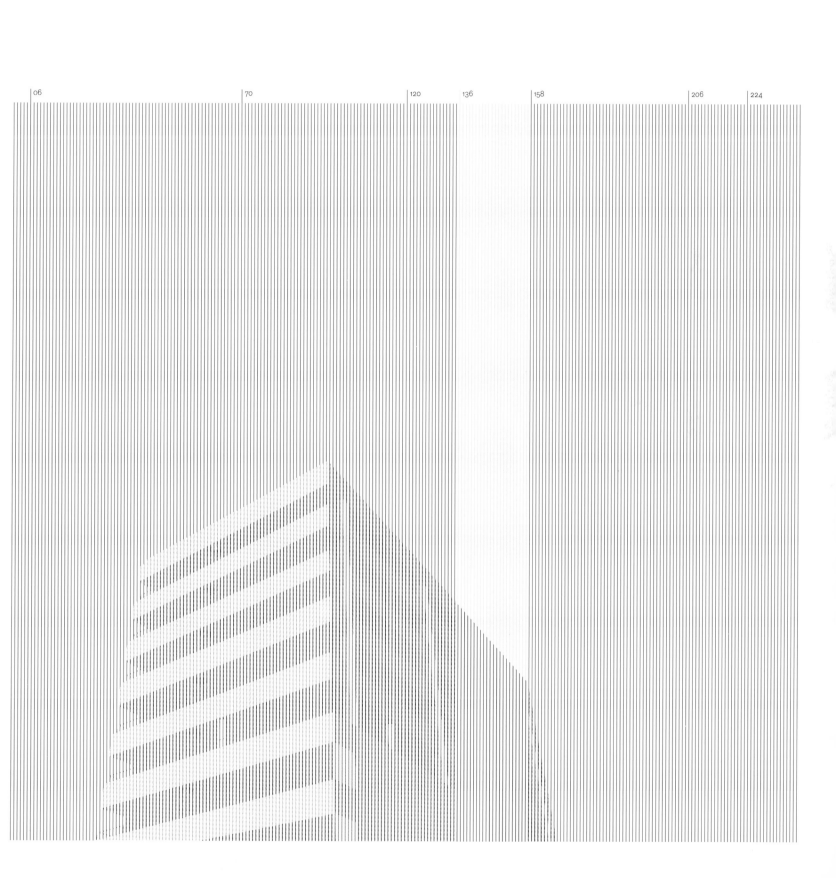

Karl Chu
In searching for a transcendent natural principle,
Chu incorporates new findings in quantum mechanics
into his designs.

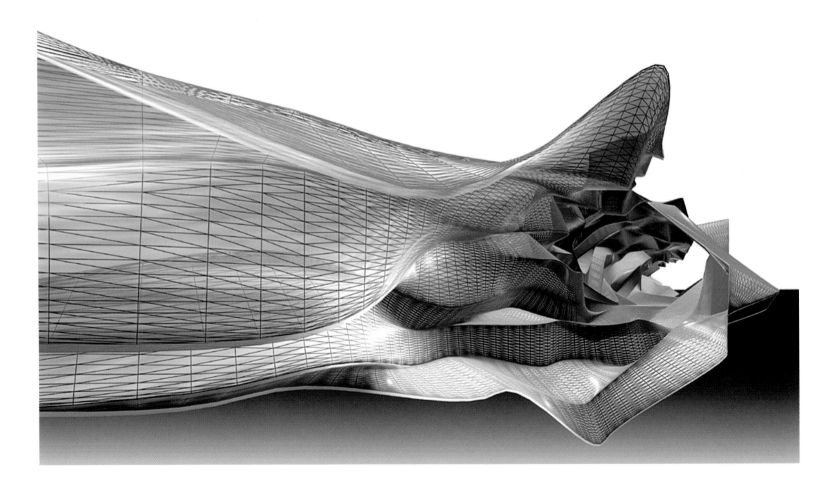

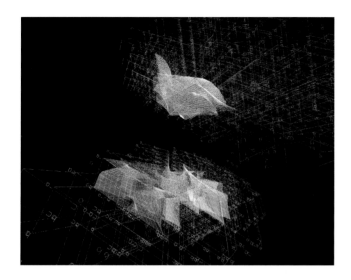

Karl Chu
Karl Chu differs from John Frazer in his attitude toward
the simulation of revolutionary processes.

LETTING THE COMPUTER LEAD

The antithesis of using the computer as a design tool, even in
such a sophisticated iteration as Frank Gehry's CATIA adaptation,
has been the radically new direction of letting the computer
guide the process. Techniques in this approach run the gamut
from John Frazer's "evolutionary paradigm" of evolving concepts
by mutating computer models in a simulated environment –
discussed at length in the introduction and represented here
by the "genetic space" of Karl S. Chu at X KAVYA, and to a
less extreme degree by Lars Spuybroek at NOX – through
the interactive explorations of young design groups in more
established offices such as Eisenman Associates, the Jerde
Partnership, and T.F. Hamzah and Yeang, to the lyrical
cybermetaphors of Toyo Ito.

The Fate of Nature

Karl S. Chu raises the issue of the transformation of nature
(initiated during the Enlightenment) through the ascendancy
of rationality that was finally realized in modernity. Chu
concentrates on the next possible stage in that process, taking
into account the changes that have taken place in quantum
mechanics, information technology, and spatial perception,
especially in relation to the concept of abstract movement.
As discussed in this book's introduction, this reference to current
investigations into human spatial perception is rare among the
growing number of "liquid architecture" zealots. But Chu focuses
on the transformation of modernity into "a cosmogenetic principle
where synthesis is the pre-eminent outcome of a return to a
second nature – a transcendent concept of nature."[72]

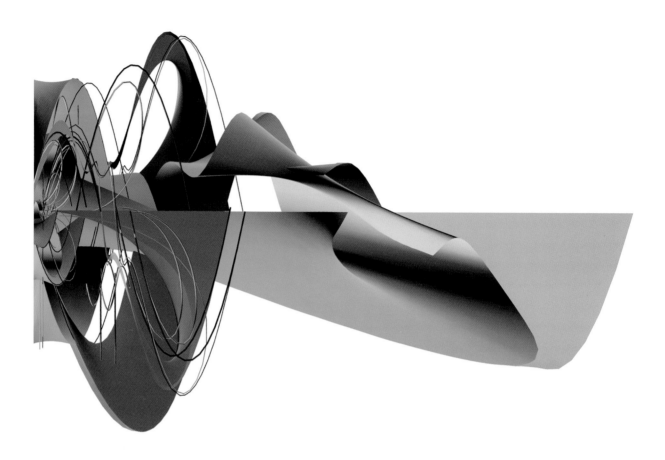

Karl Chu
Chu speaks of the synthesis of cosmogenic principles and their
continual transformation of nature.

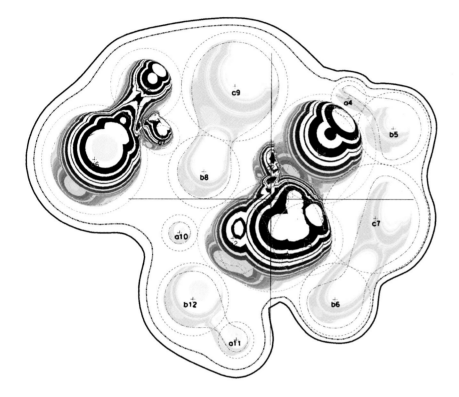

Karl Chu
Unusually, Chu's work refers to current investigations into human spatial perception.

While generically similar to the pioneering work of John Frazer and his explorations into developing a beneficially based architecture, Chu differs slightly in his emphasis on the virtual definition of genetic space, and the dominance of the algorithms unleashed to create it. He sees our species adapting in the future to an "electronically induced ethereal space" rather than electronically generating an architecture constructed from genetic codes that will allow it to conform to the existing environment, as Frazer suggests. Frazer predicts an invented, artificial ecology rather than an electronic synthesis with the real natural world we know; the inescapable inference being that its destruction is a foregone conclusion because of the theoretical deconstruction

that has preceded it. This pessimistic argument is based on the fundamental changes that have taken place in the concept of space-time, which has had and continues to have direct implications in the dimension of human reason.[73]

Chu's "genetic space" is an extension of what he characterizes as a new "cosmic conception of reason" that will evolve because of this changing awareness of space-time. He cautions that genetic space differs from the interactive formulation of images that is already generally understood as cyberspace, and that while it is also predicated on the known logic of evolutionary systems, it is "entry-level modelling of a possible world that is still in its embryonic state."

The Soft Technology of Desire

Instead of concentrating on a purely generative rationale, the Dutch firm NOX has instituted a critique of functionality which relies heavily on ideas put forward by Maurice Merleau-Ponty in *The Phenomenology of Perception*. Beginning with quantified diagrams of various kinds in a quasi-conventional brief – which they refer to as "movement in the building" – contiguous with conceptual diagrams created in the computer that are then animated by quantified data – resulting in "movement in the architecture" – NOX arrive at plotted diagrams of actual behavioral patterns – "movement in the body" – translated into space. But, they explain, this translation is not intended to be static or permanent. Rather, "the movement in the architecture is analyzed as the transformation of one architectural element into another, from floor into wall, from line into surface, from point into line… all this morphing, blending, merging, twisting, rotating, delaminating, and splitting are actions that become part of the form and create in-betweens."

Mediation, in this process, literally becomes the infusion of all material and space with media representation, with form as both the result and generator of information. Perhaps the clearest expression of this approach is a design for the New Palace Hotel on the beach at Noordwijk, the Netherlands, and a nearby boulevard, commissioned by the Amsterdam Design Institute in 1997. Trying to eliminate the linear demarcation between land, water, and sky, NOX attempted to fuse architecture and the horizon by pulling particles representing sand from the beach, or bubbles representing water, up into a vortex. The patterns of spiraling particles then became the pathways of a 460-foot- (140-meter-) high structural steel frame wrapped in a translucent, but not transparent fabric. The spatial experience NOX wanted was that of a salt water float tank, which induces weightlessness and sensory confusion because of diffused light, creating the phenomenon of polar inertia, of "being nowhere and everywhere at the same time." The hotel rooms do not connect to the outer wall, but are irregularly spaced a few meters behind it, forming a cavity wall for circulation around the perimeter and a space in which wind, rising up the vortex, is electronically amplified. The fabric wrapping the tower becomes a projection screen at night, for movies that can be seen from the beach, and sunsets are filmed, magnified, and projected from inside the tower onto the fabric, remaining there after dark.

The name that NOX has given the tower, "Beachness," could imply several things: its sandy or bubbly conception, or perhaps that it is the media equivalent of the Loch Ness monster. The name could equally mark the inversion of the usual beach hotel situation of only some of the rooms actually having an ocean view, since here the beach and sunset are inside, in a simulacrum intended to be more real than nature.

NOX: Beachness, Noordwijk
Rather than being concerned about each room having an ocean view, NOX decided to have the hotel become the ocean, by conceptually pulling it up into a vortex.

NOX: Beachness, Noordwijk
The New Palace Hotel at Noordwijk, the Netherlands, was the vehicle for the Beachness studies.

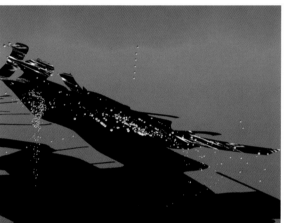

NOX: Beachness
In a reversal of most beach hotels, a translucent wrapper
projects the reflection of the ocean into the interior.

NOX: H$_2$O water pavilion, Zeeland, the Netherlands
The pavilion was designed as part of the Delta Expo
"Waterland." As in much computer-generated architecture,
translation into habitable space remains conjectural.

NOX: H$_2$O water pavilion, Zeeland, the Netherlands
A video still from inside the pavilion – an installation that does not
contain an exhibition in the classical sense.

NOX: Beachness
Once enclosed, the spiralling vortex of bubbles becomes a tower with a completely new configuration.

Jerde Partnership: Miramar, Taiwan
The challenges of bridging the gap between figurative conception and spatial reality are evident in the Miramar leisure project.

From Entertainment to Envelopment

The position of Jon Jerde as the pre-eminent practitioner of "entertainment architecture," of representing the tangible thematic equivalent of virtual space on an international urban scale, has shifted significantly. While Jerde has been a staunch advocate of exploring a concept graphically as well as providing spectacular renderings for client presentations, the new generation of designers in his office, such as Albert Vass, are using 3D Studio and CADMAX to extend the scope of those explorations in a scenario that is typical of the impact of this transitional operation on conventional practice. Vass also typifies ground zero in his attitude about letting the computer lead, or "do what it does," an acceptance of capitalizing on random events that is not the extreme position advocated by John Frazer or Karl S. Chu, but an interactive process in which the computer is recognized as an equal partner. Vass describes this as "same time realization" – seeing all contingencies at once rather than the slower, sequential, and iterative design process that preceded it. He compares the newly required talent of "recognizing accidents" involved in making a proof sheet in photography, and selecting the best image. That comparison is particularly apt, because the photographer controls the result up to a point, but the camera and the interpretive act of developing always hold surprises. The best photographers anticipate those surprises and use them to best advantage.

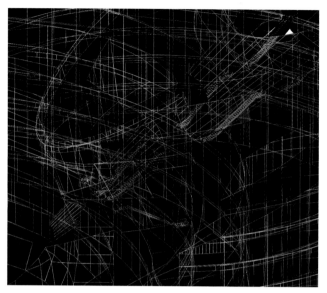

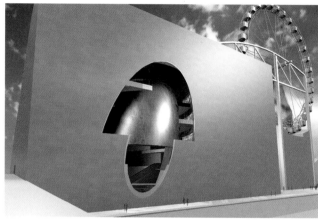

Jerde Partnership: Miramar, Taiwan
Overlays of various kinds of information helped prompt a
new direction.

Jerde Partnership: Miramar, Taiwan
The façade highlights the focus on the internal
experience that is the essence of the project.

The photographic analogy is also relevant to the advantages
the firm has recognized in presenting digital images to clients,
rather than traditional graphic renderings. Because of the
subliminal authority that electronic images now command, Vass
believes digital imagery is now seen as "photo-realistic" by clients,
who accept it as given. This transference must certainly have
been an advantage in securing approval for the Miramar project
in Taiwan. The structure comprises a multi-use Soanian double-
shell dome and oculus, with no visible means of support, which
crown an egg-shaped interior world that is carved out of a solid
block, eroded on the outside to relate to the context of the street.
In this case the iterations evident on the instantaneous contact
sheet show a subtractive process, guided by commercial lease
steps, which became the governing spatial vectors in an inside-
out sequence that stops at the envelope, treating the street
as neutral.

At Roppangi Station, the Jerde Partnership added non-axial
circulation to a masterplan previously developed by the client, the
Mori Building Company, to establish connections between single
buildings of various functions along the street. For this project the
Jerde Partnership is coordinating a team which includes Kohn
Pedersen Fox, Richard Gluckman Architects, Maki and Associates,
CD Partnership, and the landscape architects EDAW and Mark
Peter Keene. With the intention of keeping planning goals flexible
the team promoted a number of ideas, but the project's core
concept is a winding "corridor" lined with small stores that
descends 50 feet (15.2 meters) across the site to the lowest floor
containing a garden that recalls Japan's Edo period. Beginning
with an arrival "plaza" that includes a subway station, this corridor
incorporates the Jerde-designed Hollywood Cosmetics Building
and a high-rise tower by Kohn Pedersen Fox, conceptually linking
the human-made to the natural, glass tower to park.

Jerde Partnership: Roppangi Station, Tokyo
The surface of the entry tower acts as a billboard and projection screen.

Jerde Partnership: Roppangi Station, Tokyo
By stripping away the street level, the entire circulation diagram becomes visible. Digital imagery is now seen as "photo-realistic" by many clients.

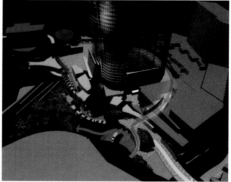

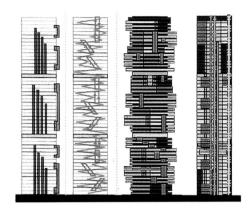

Hamzah and Yeang: Nagoya 2005 Tower
Once different systems are mapped spontaneous interaction becomes easier.

Hamzah and Yeang: BATC Tower, Setapak
By choosing to specialize in tower design, Hamzah and Yeang have more latitude in affecting typological change.

Green Cities in the Sky

While Ken Yeang and the young designers that work with him now use an interactive approach similar to that described by Vass, Yeang's passion for environmental issues introduces the paradoxical twist of a cybernetically designed, natural or sustainable architecture, primarily intended for that city. This paradox mirrors that of the architect himself; a visionary pragmatist who has sought worldwide recognition on a green mandate. Soon after returning home from the academic rigors of the Architectural Association in London and the University of Pennsylvania, where Ian McHarg influenced him a great deal, Yeang surveyed the state of affairs in his native South East Asia. He realized that for economic, symbolic, and psychological reasons, the high-rise tower is a necessary evil as the topology of choice in Asia and as such, should be humanized. He has since single-mindedly staked out this territory, all but patenting the term "sustainable skyscraper," and winning kudos for his realistic assessment of growth patterns and preferences and for his attempt to accommodate those within a sustainable ethic. Yeang's Menara Messinaga won an Aga Khan Award for Architecture because of its natural ventilation strategies – even though a Teflon-coated fiberglass wind scoop at the top, intended to funnel prevailing breezes into an atrium core, has yet to be implemented – and because the architect addressed diurnal differences in solar angle in the positioning of sunshading bands and in the location of visible, rather than merely decorative, balconies. The

UMNO party headquarters in Penang, Malaysia, is an even more proactive statement of the need to lower energy costs by supplementing air conditioning with natural ventilation. A huge, vertical, fin-like "wind-wing-wall" is strategically positioned to catch high breezes and funnel them through all the offices.

Yeang's Nagoya 2005 tower intentionally takes these ideas to extremes in order both to test the limits of incorporating vegetation into tower technology and to dramatize the saving of arable land that can be achieved by going vertical. The main function of the computer here has been in optimizing climatic benefit and calculating structural loads and feasibility. However, in the case of the Business Advancement Technology Center, a low-rise research and development complex in Setapak, Malaysia, the designers used the computer more intuitively to integrate built form and landscape into an intricately patterned collage.

Post-occupancy performance research on completed projects has yet to catch up to the rapid implementation of such sustainable principles, which was made possible by the economic growth in Asia prior to the 1997 crash. With recovery slowly but surely underway, making it probable that Yeang will be able to expand his empirical base, the necessity for follow-up documentation becomes even more critical, an opportunity waiting to be seized.

Hamzah and Yeang: Nagoya 2005 Tower
The Nagoya Tower represents the culmination of many ideas
that have been developed by the firm over the last decade.

Hamzah and Yeang: BATC Tower, Setapak
The BATC Tower dominates low-rise components around it, in
a complex intended to advance business related technologies.

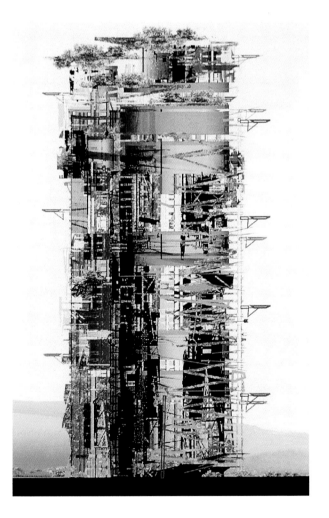

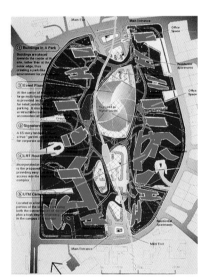

Toyo Ito: Mediatheque, Sendai
The columns woven between the slabs of this combined art gallery, library, and audiovisual center replicate fiberoptic cable.

Toyo Ito: Mediatheque, Sendai
The interior of one of the thirteen funnel-like columns that support the Mediatheque.

Toyo Ito: Mediatheque, Sendai
Utilities and communications systems are threaded
through the lattices.

Toyo Ito: Mediatheque, Sendai
The distance between the slabs varies, to simulate
computer chip lamination.

The Mediatheque is the Message

Computer technology has sometimes been a figurative as well
as a literal inspiration in design, providing compelling imagery
that architects attempt to replicate. The Mediatheque by Toyo Ito
in Sendai, Japan, had a difficult brief — including an art gallery,
library, and audiovisual facility — which the architect has dealt
with in a disarmingly simple way. Deciding to convey the idea of
a media center by capturing its ethereal essence in a reductive
palette of materials, Ito set additional limits on the kinds of
elements he would use by selecting the archetypes of plates,
tubes, and skin. The plates are seven square slabs, stacked in
a variety of floor heights to give the impression of lamination,
with each intended to symbolize "a different mode of
communication between people and between people and things
through different types of media. The height of each tier defined
by the plates differs from one floor to another, but the plates
are interchangeable." The tubes are woven into 13 tree-like
funnels that support the floor plates and also accommodate

vertical circulation, utilities, and communications. The main street
of Sendai, which runs in front of the building, is known for its
zelkova trees. The funnels are at once abstract replicants of
these trees and of fiberoptic cables. The glass skin, delicately
etched in a pattern that implies circuitry, is actually a cavity wall
that allows natural ventilation to flow between two sheets of
glass, continuing the natural-artificial interface.

The implications of the symbolism used in the Mediatheque
— of being inside a computer chip, of becoming the technology
we use, of the growing lack of privacy that it is causing, equated
with its complete transparency — are made far less frightening
by its cold, erotic beauty. Taken together, Ito's archetypes add
up to an analog of scientific alchemy: the human yearning to
replace corporal fragility with technologically enhanced longevity
and perfection figuratively realized in the frigid envelope of
the Mediatheque.

Unmasking the Intention of Scientific Method

The imagery of Ito's cables also shows up in Peter Eisenman's entry in the Musée du Quai Branly competition, one of a series of recent projects that have signaled a new focus and authority in this architect's work. While the competition was won by Jean Nouvel, Eisenman's runner-up scheme remains an important commentary on the same symbolic issues that Ito has eloquently captured, with layered permutations related to location and proposed function that add profound insights to the message of the Mediatheque. Located on the Left Bank, just north of the Eiffel Tower and the Champs de Mars, Eisenman's museum, to house the tribal collection of the Musée d'Ethnographie du Trocadéro, consists of interwoven strands that seem to be extruded from the existing buildings that bracket the elongated, gently curving riverfront site. Ito's "tubes" at Sendai celebrate the final transcendence of scientific method, representing fiberoptic conduits of pure information that will inevitably and progressively replace their imperfect organic equivalent. Eisenman's convoluted strands proclaim the inversion of the imperial world order that this methodology was fabricated to maintain. His proposal for the Musée du Quai Branly is the architectural equivalent of *Les demoiselles d'Avignon* — inspired by the tribal masks Picasso saw at the Musée de l'Ethnographie — which was intended to confound Western conventions of representation. Eisenman uses the form of a twisted mask, as it would appear from the top of the Eiffel Tower, as a symbol of the non-European cultures which have been exploited by colonialism, confronting the convention of the Cartesian grid — the ubiquitous urban inheritance of the French Enlightenment — and that of the museum as institutional evidence of the rationalist's obsession with categories. The warped roof surfaces, supported by the kind of open cross-braced frame structure usually associated with roller coasters, are intended as a park, a reprise of the replacement of nature by technology that Bernard Tschumi implemented at la Villette, and reminder of Eisenman's catalytic role in introducing French critic Jacques Derrida and the subsequent phase of deconstructivism to the architectural profession and the public. Unlike la Villette, however, where trees and grass were to be replaced by steel, concrete, and asphalt as a parable of the final extinction of the environment, Eisenman planned to locate landscaped gardens in valleys between the sloping roof strands as a marked retreat from complete technological destruction.

**Peter Eisenman: Musée du Quai Branly,
Paris, competition entry**
The extruded strands that unravel to become the museum
represent the evolution of a new world order.

**Peter Eisenman: Staten Island Institute Center
for Electronic Culture**
This museum represents overlays of information about
the transportation systems that converge here.

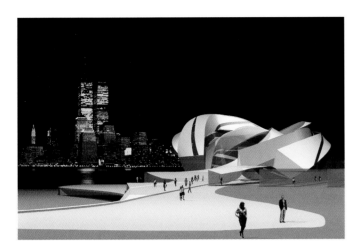

**Peter Eisenman: Staten Island Institute
Center for Electronic Culture**
The cybernetic revolution is legible in the design
of the Center, which celebrates it.

By replacing the binary Cartesian figure-ground pattern with this organic alternative, Eisenman also calls into question the either-or basis of artificial intelligence and its synonym in digital design, which was obviously a necessary component in establishing the complicated curves and intricate contortions of his projects shown here. Such critical humanism signifies a substantial shift in direction for an architect best known for his reliance on abstract, theoretical sources, and accounts for the depth and resonance evident here. [74]

Like the Mediatheque in Sendai, the Staten Island Institute Center for Electronic Culture spatially and formally describes the information revolution that is celebrated by the exhibits within. Eisenman's new museum, to be built next to and partially above the St. George terminal of the Staten Island ferry at the mouth of New York Harbor, is functionally tied to the terminal building and reflects all of the transportation systems that converge there: the trains, buses, and cars that, in addition to the ferry piers and platforms, surround the site. Using the same process introduced at the Wexner Center for Art in Columbus, Ohio – where the dimensions of the street grid and the foundation footprint of a pre-existing Armory were the basis for the architect's intervention of a three-dimensional framework – Eisenman has extruded a two-dimensional grid marking major topographic features on Staten Island, and has overlayed information about the various transportation systems on it to derive the museum. This process,

of formulating a datascape and superimposing a mnemonic map of functionally or historically relevant counterpoints on it, intentionally precludes any associations with arbitrary expressionistic or metaphorical precedents. It also cannot technically be called Contexualism since it involves a digitally devised sublimation rather than abstract or literal translation of adjacencies. [75]

Unlike the Mediatheque, which, with its uncanny resemblance to a habitable silicon chip, is arguably more metaphorical, the Center for Electronic Culture carefully adheres to rational tradition, as a prerequisite for both a subliminal and visceral lesson in the causal relationship between the scientific method that grew out of that tradition and the cybernetic revolution that the museum represents. With its Infohall, which soars 44 feet (13 meters) above entry level, and which is being promoted by borough leaders as an "Electronic Town Square," its five long galleries full of interactive exhibitions and digital library, along with the requisite financial support of restaurant and bookstore, the Center is a true museum for the twenty-first century, inviting the tourists, which Staten Island now needs, to fully experience information in the architecture and exhibits.

chapter 4
corrupting the media:
graphic/digital hybrids

158

Eric Owen Moss: Culver City, aerial view
It is rare for an architect to have the opportunity to work in an extensive part of a major metropolitan area for a long period of time, as Moss has in Culver City.

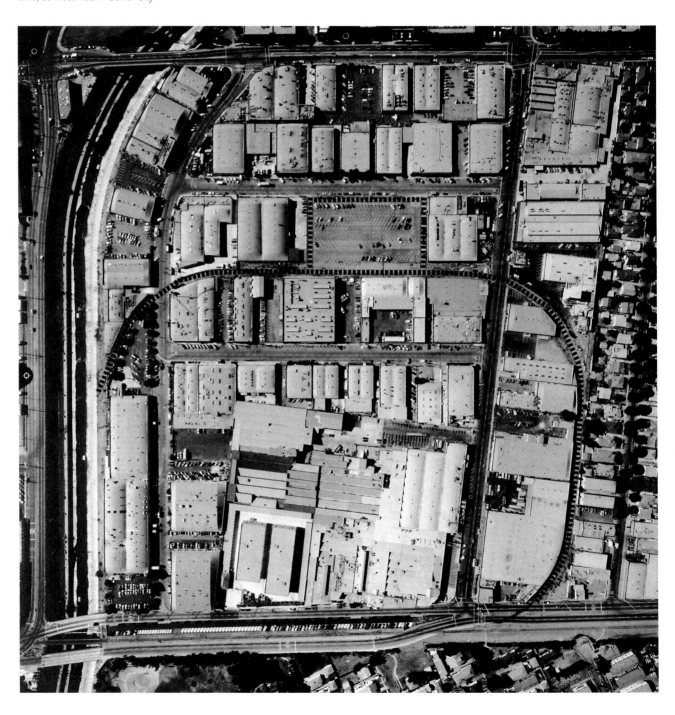

Eric Owen Moss: Culver City, Los Angeles
The concrete-lined Los Angeles river is an apt metaphor for the
hard-edged urban realities Eric Moss is attempting to accommodate.

CORRUPTING THE MEDIA: GRAPHIC / DIGITAL HYBRIDS

Computing has undeniably accelerated design and construction
time, but paradoxically, the long-proclaimed advent of leisure
time that it was supposed to make possible has not happened
and the length of the average workday has actually increased.
This has also resulted in a new kind of workplace, where an
electronically skilled family of workers are joined together in
collective isolation inside digital cities. Rather than resembling
the suburban or exurban vision that many planners describe, of
gleeful, "outsourced" employees connected by modem to their
increasingly temporary office from the comfort of their home,
this collective is configured to feed on productive synergy by
employers who are reluctant to relinquish visual control.

Eric Moss and His Digital City

Because he has had the unusual opportunity of being affiliated
with a developer who owns a great deal of real estate in Culver
City, west of Los Angeles, Eric Moss has single-handedly been
attempting to define the graphic/digital hybrid genre.

Frederick Smith, who is Moss's partner, patron, or client,
depending on how their professional relationship is characterized,
inherited his father's property in Culver City, a section known as
the Hayden Tract, in 1987. Smith had been working in Europe
in the early 1970s when his father's declining health had made it
necessary for him to return home to manage the family business,
the most challenging aspect of which was this industrial tract.
By the early 1980s, industrial decline in the United States, due
to high costs, overheads, and wages, as well as government
regulations, was well established. The transition from an industrial
to a service-based or information economy was underway.
Smith was trying his best to make it through this period of
transition and realized that he had to:

> find a way to attract the new kinds of companies that could
> replace the fleeing industrialists. I knew there was a huge
> sector of new business based on soft-tech applications of
> technology and felt that if we were entering a technical
> revolution as fundamental as the industrial revolution was to
> an agrarian society, wouldn't a tenant, if given a choice, want
> a building without an antiquated, nostalgic environment?

Smith saw the large industrial sheds that already existed in the Hayden Tract as a bridge between these two eras of industrial and information-based economy, and began looking for an architect who shared his vision to help him realize it. After many interviews he met Eric Moss, who was a tenant. Smith found that he and Moss shared similar tastes in literature and art, and they began their collaboration on the Paramount Laundry conversion in 1987, followed by 8522 National in the same year. These first renovations set the tone of the partnership: existing industrial buildings, many with the wooden "bow-string" trusses that are characteristics of such construction in the 1920s and 1930s, were stripped to the structural bone and recreated in the partners' image of a new internally oriented, electronically focused world. Since the Paramount and 8522 National projects, there have been more than a dozen others, either designed, now in construction, or completed, with the Pittard Sullivan complex being the most recent example of the latter. These have acquired titles of their own in an office lexicon that is as abstract as the artificial intelligence celebrated in the architecture it designates. The buildings that have been completed since the Paramount Laundry and 7522 National, for example, are named the Lindblade Tower (1988), Gary Group (1990), the Box (1994), IRS (1994), Samitaur (1996), Pittard Sullivan (1998), the Green Umbrella and appendages (1999), and Stealth, now underway.

Realistic Topologies

In addition, Smith and Moss have pursued the acquisition of the remainder of the air rights over the Southern Pacific Railroad that cuts a half-mile-long swath through the Hayden Tract and is only partially owned by Smith. The partners have named this Southern Pacific Air Rights (S.P.A.R.) City and plan that it will join together many of these existing and proposed projects adding mass transportation, housing, and parks as the final components in the city of the future that they envision. The significant thing about each of the pieces in this intricate puzzle is that they are in an existing context and have been redesigned to remain so, rather than being put forward as an alternative to it. The modernist tactic of bulldozing in order to start with a clean slate is not operational here. Moss has deliberately approached each of the projects in the Hayden Tract as a didactic opportunity to create a more realistic urban prototype, one that is able to accommodate the city as it is. Following the mass desertion at the end of the industrial age, many cities in the Western world are shrinking rather than growing. The digital entrepreneurs that have replaced the inner city manufacturing giants have chosen cheaper and more flexible accommodations on the fringe of the city and in suburban areas, and Los Angeles has one of the largest conglomerations of such digital enterprises in the United States. Moss believes that working within the abandoned fabric of the post-industrial city and accepting the old freeways, wide surface streets, parking lots, warehouse sheds, and concrete and steel towers as a challenging reality, rather than a constructional nuisance to be torn up or down first, makes sense on several levels. Primarily, it is good business because the digital pioneers that Smith and Moss want to attract are young and politically correct. The idea of conservation, of participating in a piece of history, is as appealing to them as having their company identified with an architectural work of art. The extent of such conservation is tempered by fiscal constraints on the developer's side, since it usually costs more to save an old building than to bulldoze it and begin again. In the buildings completed in the Hayden Tract this conservation ranges from the token replacement of several elements to the determined preservation of the majority of an existing structure. Pittard Sullivan falls somewhere near the middle of this scale, but even so, it does not conform in the slightest to the conventions of preservation confirmed by the Venice Charter. Moss usually leaves no nail unpulled, dismantling most of a structure, cleaning and repairing the parts that can be salvaged, and re-erecting them in similar or different configurations, which are symbolically important to him.

Eric Owen Moss: Pittard Sullivan
Moss has used computer technology to enhance rather
than replace his own exceptional three-dimensional sense.

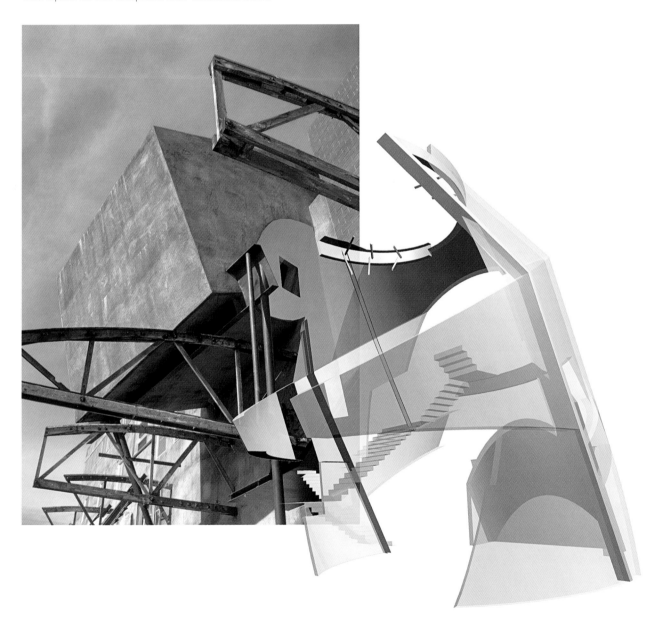

Eric Owen Moss: S.P.A.R. City, Los Angeles
Each of the projects Moss designs are intended to be part of the
new city (the name comes from Southern Pacific Air Rights) that
he is creating, west of the center of Los Angeles.

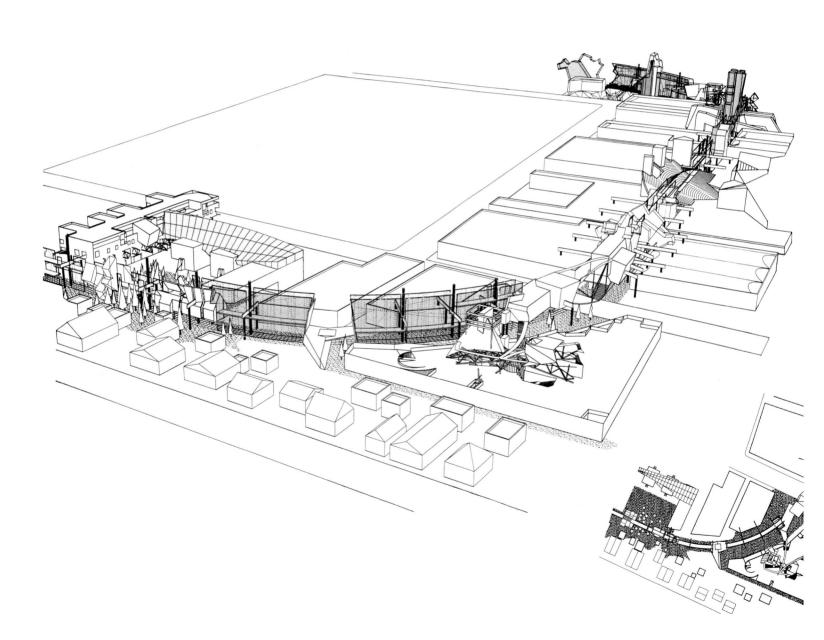

The second reason that Moss accepts the reality of existing context, which will confound even his severest critics, is to show that such recycling need not be antithetical to the concept of the architectural avant garde, or put more conventionally, that sustainability can also be hip. Usually associated in the public consciousness with the ecology movement of the late 1960s and early 1970s, sustainability is a radical expansion of it, encompassing world resource depletion, global politics, and the balance of trade and debt as related to those resources, the efficiency of the building techniques used by traditional societies, concepts of mixed use to increase density, reduced automobile dependency, and maximum energy conservation. It only marginally supports the continued exploration of the solar technologies previously associated with environmental architecture. Because of its integral association with resource conservation, as examined at length by the British physicist Dr. Ian Boustead, material recycling plays an integral part in the efficacy of sustainability, but most architects are reluctant to deal with it because it requires more care and detailed tracking than conventional tracking and conventional construction techniques. While usually related to the materials themselves in Boustead's studies – such as the recycling of aluminum or steel to reduce the use of bauxite or iron ore and the extreme levels of energy they originally require to produce – recycling in Moss's case is more a matter of attitude than a significant savings in resources. The wooden bow-string trusses that are the centerpiece of his recycling efforts do not also represent a threatened resource, since pine is regenerative and sustainably correct, but their unique function as artifacts of a factory culture in a city with precious few historical artifacts contributes to their scarcity.

The third, more general, reason Moss has for working with the existing Culver City context is that it is more realistic to do so, in the sense of providing urban topologies for the future that represent real paragons for Los Angeles. LA is generally considered to be an accurate predictor of the way the growing global megalopolis is going and the so-called "catalytic projects" of the city's newly released Downtown Strategic Plan conform to a conventional planner's image of the public realm of the sort drawn by Gordon Cullen in the 1960s: parks and riverside quays filled with happy balloon-carrying people, farmers' markets, streets full of shoppers, theaters, and museums with more of the same, all supposedly contributing to the fulfillment of the contemporary vision of the *res publica*. As an alternative, Moss offers disturbing models for buildings that straddle freeways, partially accommodate or engulf existing factories and warehouses, weave around and through industrial concrete or steel towers, incorporate rather than ignore parking lots, and accept the harsh truth of an increasingly interior, computer-dominated digital world.

In an article in *Los Angeles Magazine* entitled "Digital City," in which LA was praised as the perfect place for creating false realities, the hidden extent of electronic entrepreneurship was exposed. "According to a study conducted by the Bay Area Economic Forum," the article reveals, "LA multimedia firms employ 133,000 people – more than the combined total of those in the field in New York and the Bay area [the northern California counties surrounding San Francisco], each of which employs roughly 60,000." [76] The Forum's figures include CD-Rom, virtual imaging, Web page design, and other internet-based entertainment industries. Similar studies confirm LA's dominance in cyberindustry, with 45 of the 80 top multimedia producers in the United States located there and other, more highly publicized media cities, such as Seattle, Washington, and Austin, Texas, only representing a portion of the action that LA now has. The city's long-established position as a film and television production center has helped to ensure that prominence, and Culver City is the eye of the storm. The Hayden Tract, which the article describes as

Eric Owen Moss: Pittard Sullivan, Los Angeles
The provision of vertical circulation space has provided a good opportunity for
sculptural expression in all of Moss's Culver City conversions.

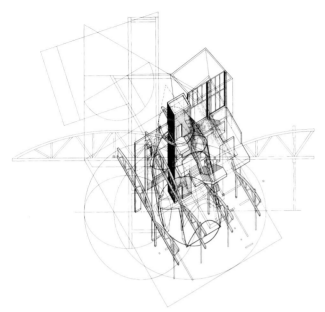

Eric Owen Moss: Pittard Sullivan
In the design for the office building various kinds of
information are superimposed to condense meaning.

"a 57-acre [23-hectare] zone of mostly vacant brick buildings
dating back to the aerospace boom of the 40s and 50s," was the
perfect symbol of LA's sudden post-Cold War industrial
obsolescence. "By the early 90s, as military contracts dried up
and aerospace companies downsized," it explains, "employment in
the district, once a bustling 4,000, dwindled to less than 500."
Frederick Smith and Eric Moss have largely been responsible for
this renaissance, which many believe is just beginning. Pittard
Sullivan is recognized as a leader in the digital imaging world and
their tenancy in the Hayden Tract continues a who's who list that
also includes Cyber Studios, Digital Planet, and W3 Design,
among about 30 others, with a total of more than 2,000
employees. It is a good example of the Smith-Moss approach, and
of these new cyber environments.

Four Iterations of Pittard Sullivan:
Digital Birth of a Digital Empire
Because of the transitory nature of the new breed of tenant
that Smith and Moss hope to attract, the design process that the
developer wants to encourage is frequently interrupted. Moss
euphemistically describes the situation as being "in flux," because
'clients don't come in with big machines anymore and set them
up for a 30-year run. Those people and that vision of the world
are gone and no one really knows what the new basis of the
economy really is. Communities like Culver City are desperate to
find tax support to keep municipal services operating." This has
required Moss to be extremely flexible and the Pittard Sullivan
project is a definitive example of the diverse approach this new
situation requires, generating a verbal shorthand all its own.

Pittard Sullivan began as a headquarters for Rhino Records,
or R1 in Moss shorthand, an existing east-west oriented 240-
foot- (73-meter-) long rectangular warehouse with a roof carried
on 13 parallel pairs of bow-string trusses, fronted by a U-shaped
piece that included a tower. Moss removed the roof of the
rectangular warehouse and demolished the U-shaped piece and
tower in the front. The pairs of bow-string trusses and their
supporting columns were refurbished and left standing, following
a precedent already established at 8522 National Boulevard,
completed in 1988. A steel frame of tube columns and wide
flange beams was then inserted as an orthogonal system around
the trusses to carry three office floors. The center column of
the typical bow-string truss falls in the middle of a double loaded
corridor running through the middle of the office block. The
southern limit of the linear frame falls inside the second pair of
trusses, which project past it. Moss has cut these off at various
lengths and they gradually extend to accentuate the entrance.
The next design move was to insert four long walls which the
architect describes as beginning on the south perimeter where
the first wall accommodates the parking dimension on the side.
"Car, aisle, double car, aisle, car, wall. That starts the building,
ipso facto. I had to get the cars in." This was followed by two
parallel interior walls which define the circulation system as a
double-height volume, and, lastly there is an exterior wall on
the north perimeter.

Eric Owen Moss: Pittard Sullivan
One bay of an existing warehouse was removed, allowing
the trusses that supported it to project out in a defensive
line toward the parking lot.

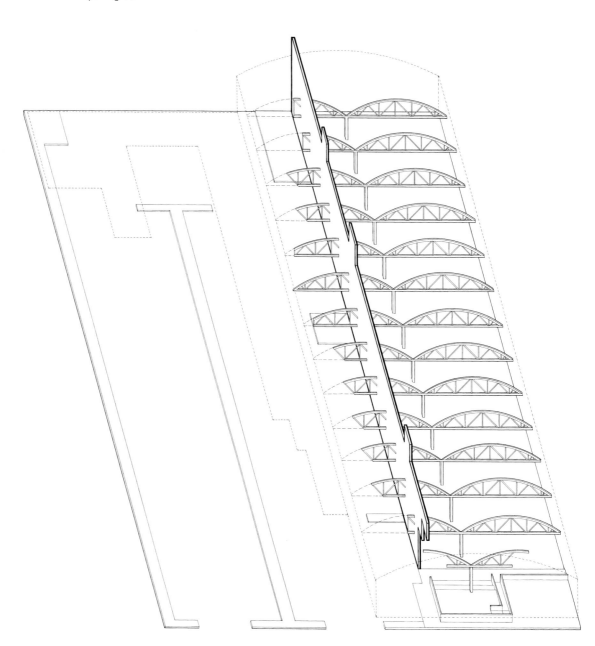

All external surfaces of the building are naturally enclosed, so Moss's way of conceptualizing the design – as a steel frame inserted over a series of existing bow trusses followed by a parallel series of four linear walls – is very revealing as an explanation of his view of the role of architecture in this circumstance. His unprecedented attempt to conform to, rather than obliterate, existing pieces of urban detritus has generated a new methodology of thinking in terms of the interrelationship of staged systems and the walls he describes as "incremental planes that mark the gradual transition from an external, automobile-oriented to an internal, digitally controlled world." Rather than considering the parking lot an open storage facility for cars, he gives it a more generative function of "starting the building." It is a reminder of the central role given to the parking lot in the Paramount Laundry, Lindblade Towers, and the Gary Group complex, comparable to an Angeleno Italian Piazza for the Nineties, in which cars have replaced people as the center of attention. Cars, as Moss indicates, are "ipso facto" in spite of all attempts by new urbanists to wish them away or legislate them into oblivion. The policy decision made in Los Angeles after World War II, to build freeways at the expense of public transportation, has had profound repercussions for the city. One of the first cities in North America to have a railway, affectionately remembered as the "Red Cars," Los Angeles is now struggling through an unusually dark bureaucratic abyss to build a subway and to upgrade its antiquated bus system, which is a constant source of local media criticism. Complaints generally focus on overcrowded conditions, lack of recognition of the socioeconomic status of the ridership, relatively high fares, and frequency of service in lower-income areas. These intractable difficulties support the theory that automobiles will continue to be the personal transport of choice for the foreseeable future, so ingrained in the Los Angeles lifestyle because of the freedom it offers and the status it has come to convey. Rather than considering what might be, Moss deals with this reality as it is, and designs to accommodate it. Two further iterations followed, from an international competition for a house (dubbed R2), which Moss decided should resemble the Rhino Records Lobby, followed by a theater configuration at one corner of the rectangular massing, the R3 Theater. The competition graphics for R2, the house, are an elegant virtual collaging of layers that have a silk-screen quality, focusing on the tapering center volume only, with the wings extending out on either side deleted. The competition involved providing a concept for an ideal, fantasy residence on any site chosen by the architect and the significant aspect of Moss's choice of the Rhino Record cum the Pittard Sullivan lobby for his submission, is that he obviously considers it domestic in character. He has compared the lobby – which he says the Pittard Sullivan is "all about" – to the core of his Lawson Westen house, one of the few residences he has realized because of his intense involvement in the Culver City experiment. The R2 house, appearing in graphic form like a colorized x-ray of the lobby, reveals the Lawson Westen cone in the middle, sliced open at a diagonal to show its insides.

Eric Owen Moss: Pittard Sullivan
Opposite: Recycled wood bow-string trusses
intentionally penetrate the new façade of Pittard
Sullivan, like a phalanx protecting it from intruders.

Below: A tilted block, hovering over the exposed
trusses, announces the entrance.

This x-ray quality is critical to an understanding of the architect's attitude toward the Pittard Sullivan design and why iteration is a more accurate term than evolution. In Moss's own words, "The second permutation is a house, R2, produced for an exhibition, which confirms the principle that the meaning of a building always precedes or supersedes its current use and is more durable than its current utility. The label 'house' didn't interest me. I just saw R2 as an exception to the R system, the interruption in the frame, an anomaly that is assigned the label of house. Ancillary pieces that abet the function of the office building are gone. The frame is removed; the trusses remain and the free truss ends are supported on pipes. R2 is a different color; we called it Peanut Butter House because that conjures up something homey, so nobody would be terrorized." To explain the dichotomy of exposing the interior of the non-house domestic design to the outside by glazing the perimeter, Moss simply says, "It is no longer just an introverted space, the volumes are now understandable from the outside. The anomaly no longer exists because the lobby was an exception to the consistency of the long office block, now removed. In R1 the office block was a foil for the lobby, now, no foil." Lastly, and perhaps most importantly, he explains about iteration that "none of the pieces in this series, R1, R2, R3, or PS, has the external power of Samitaur or the Hayden Tower. The project is more introverted. The series is as much about evolution as about form, but the evolution is not Darwinian, it's a xerox job: one building is four buildings."

It is curiously appropriate that Moss has conceptualized Pittard Sullivan as a "xerox job," rather than a design that has incrementally changed according to circumstance, in the functional modernist sense. It has been created by the same electronic processes as those used by the tenants that occupy it. The unexpected changes in use that occur in the volatile commercial market have prevented consistent development of Pittard Sullivan, unlike the Samitaur project, which was approached on a speculative basis, without a specific client in mind, and which Moss feels has more "power."

The questions that Moss's equation of residence with office core raises are compelling, assuming that it was not chosen as the competition submission out of sheer expediency, with one conclusion being the office's role as a home away from home for the digital community. Factory hours in the industrial past were set and the suburbs really were bedroom communities only a convenient commuting distance away. Digital enterprises place more demands on their employees and the length of a workday can vary according to deadlines, with 18-hour days, or more, being frequently necessary. The lack of customary urban amenities such as restaurants, cafés, or parks near the Hayden Tract development means that much of this time is spent indoors, with lunches and dinners delivered. The lobby is the one communal space in the building, the domestic equivalent for the collective enterprise.

Eric Owen Moss: Pittard Sullivan
Axonometrics show the permutations involved in
transforming an existing warehouse into the new facility.

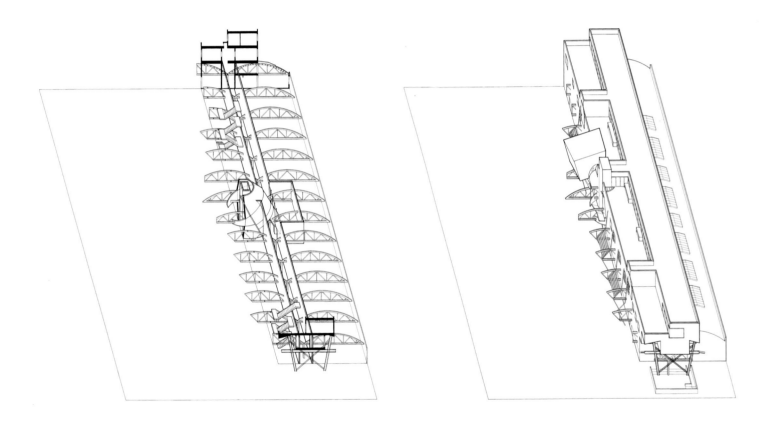

Eric Owen Moss: Pittard Sullivan
Working with developers is frequently difficult for
architects; Moss has found a formula that works.

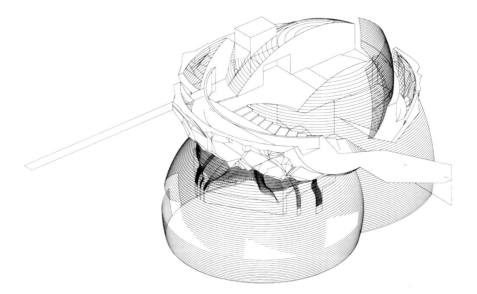

Eric Owen Moss: Pittard Sullivan
The distinction between virtual image and reality is becoming
increasingly blurred.

Eric Owen Moss: Ince Boulevard Theater
Frederick and Laurie Smith intend on using new types of
theaters to enliven the new city they call "Conjunctive Points."

The lines between work and home, once so clearly drawn
by the freeway that connected or separated them, are now
completely blurred, as the office has become home for many
people in this business. "The lobby," Moss explains, "is an anomaly,
outside the orthogonal order of steel and wood, as is the parking
lot elevation, the conference room behind the lobby and the
tipped block conference space on the second floor which are
all exceptions to the frame. The lobby is complicated, but not
unrelated to the Lawson Westen house as a spatial experiment.
Both began with a category of geometry which is recognizable
and ends up as a super, not supra geometry. The lobby is an
object-volume leaning into the south wall and cut at the exterior
building face, like a fossil. The shape presses against the front
wall and leaves its imprint as a glass aperture. Inside the lobby
there are bridges to each floor level from the black block elevator
core. The curved lobby wall extends inside to outside, crossing
the exterior wall and intersecting the tipped block. The imprint
of the south elevation is the lobby in section, elevation as section.
Inside, you get the volume: the first, second and third floor are
the outside on the inside, but never present the shape of the
outside elevation in its entirety."

The third iteration, including the Ince Boulevard Theater
as part of the complex, was part of Frederick and Laurie Smith's
initiative to return this section of Culver City more directly to
entertainment use. The R3 Theater idea did not last long, but
while it did, the lobby was extended to become the public
entrance to the theater and a private entrance to the offices,
showing its persistent central function in the designer's concept.

Moss sees R3 "as an act of contrition that brings to the public
what always was a public space. R1 had an enormous lobby
reserved for a private few. Like most of the work we've done in
Culver City, the lobby was intended for the office tenant. The first
argument for the theater was that the public would walk through
that space. The public space becomes public." In this iteration, the
lobby acts as a double valve that directs theatergoers to the east,
and office workers to the west. The theater spirals out of and up
from the orthogonal circulation, interlocking with it in a way that
explains the geometric nature of each system but doesn't allow
either one to predominate. In this iteration, the tilting box over
the lobby remains, but the projecting trusses disappear to allow
the two systems to read more clearly. Moss attempted to have
the two systems "work off each other in equity, rather than having
the theater be an anomaly, since an anomaly is an exception to a
system, one that predominates." The intention was that the
trusses would be reintroduced, but not in such an explicit way
because of the delicate balance between the circular and
orthogonal geometrics. All that prevented the developer and
architect from taking the scheme further was the site; the size
that the theater had to be for commercial viability made it exceed
property restrictions, making it more feasible to move it to
Ince Boulevard.

In the fourth and final iteration, Pittard Sullivan, the building returns to completely office use, but is enlarged by attaching four new rectilinear projections to the north wall, with louvered screens and bridges connecting the projections. The blocks on the north side have expanded the square footage from 30,000 to 50,000 (2,800 to 4,600 square meters) and are predominantly used for mechanical equipment, which is the reason for the louvers. In this fourth iteration, Moss explains, "the lobby is more complicated. In R1 there was a first floor and pieces of a second floor, accessed only by stairs, then a third level. The second floor of Pittard Sullivan is continuous, so I have introduced a new bridge in the lobby, along with a stair that connects the second and third floors."

The skin of the Pittard Sullivan building is as equally experimental as the determination of demarcation between internal and external surfaces, as befits its role of non-containment and challenging conventions. Early projects, such as the Gary Group, for example, have walls made of easily recognizable materials: brick, block, steel, and aluminum that are combined in unusual ways. The references that Moss quotes are Meso-American and the resulting massiveness is decidedly Mayan, even though the quotes are not literally executed. The Pittard Sullivan walls are made of concrete block, but are covered with steel-troweled stucco with color added, giving the surface

the appearance of a Hollywood backdrop or a Jasper Johns painting. The result is that the wall is dematerialized or virtualized, and lacks the usual associations of mass and gravitational responsibility that typical walls convey. As the architectural equivalent of the tempera technique used by Leonardo da Vinci on *The Last Supper*, the use of color in stucco has yet to be perfected, but its insubstantial appearance and subliminal scenographic associations suit Moss's purpose of rewriting the rules in a context with such strong connections to Hollywood's past and electronically enhanced future. The visual effect on the building's surface is strangely akin to that of a billboard painted as a cloud-filled sky on the Universal Studio's lot that is a favourite background scene for movie companies because the typically pollution-filled turquoise-blue Los Angeles sky rarely has clouds and so doesn't look normal to the majority of the movie watching world. Another unmistakable reference is the heavy metal Battlestar Galactica look favored by artistic directors of films such as *Independence Day*, the surface of the spacecraft models unchanged since the *Star Wars* trilogy introduced the look in the 1970s.

Eric Owen Moss: Ince Boulevard Theater
New, experimental layouts are being implemented to alter
the theatrical experience. This graphic features a
computer overlay and a photograph of the existing site.

Eric Owen Moss: Pittard Sullivan
In contrast to a spiky entrance, the rear façade responds
to the peaks and valleys of distant mountains.

This surface treatment has been criticized as being superficial or insubstantial, but the critics have missed the point that this is intentional, in keeping with the intangible, virtual nature of the entertainment industry itself. The paradox, once again, which is the equivalent of the play between inner and outer boundaries mentioned in regard to the protruding trusses, is the irreconcilable references to the sky on one hand and military heavy metal on the other, the same paradox that characterizes Los Angeles itself. Frank Gehry attempts – or attempted prior to the time that international commissions lured him out of Los Angeles in the early 1980s – to capture the essence of the city in fragmentation and collage, projecting the scenographic reference into abstracted villages or single local topologies as mundane as a lifeguard station converted into an office in a Venice Beach house to remind the owner of the carefree days of youth. But Eric Moss attacks the more basic aspect of climate, the atmosphere that makes Los Angeles different, the juxtaposition of mountains, ocean, and desert and the impressive number of rain-free days that drew migrants and film makers here in the first place. Like the majority of his most recent work, Pittard Sullivan is a serious commentary on the irony involved in living and working in one of the most benign environments in the world and yet disregarding it, focusing on an alternative reality. The Lawson Westen house, which provided the model for the Pittard Sullivan lobby, has a core that symbolizes this irony, the Piranesian quality of the stair reminiscent of the *Carceri* or prison series in which the eighteenth-century Italian artist explored new ways of expressing three-dimensionality in graphic form. The house, as prison in a beautiful climate, has come about as a result of Los Angeles' evolving role as an international gateway, replacing the role that New York served at the end of the nineteenth century. From people moving to Los Angeles from all over the United States as a result of land speculation in the early 1900s, the dustbowl catastrophe in the 1920s, and in search of a more relaxed lifestyle immediately after World War II, the city has now become the preferred destination of outside immigration, predominantly from the south or west. The unprecedented social mixture pouring into the city has produced paranoia in WASP enclaves, such as those on the West Side, where the Lawson Westen house is located, intermittently reinforced by riots, hovering helicopters, and atrocious crimes that seem to occur with disturbing frequency. The natural wonders and calamities that awed earlier architects, encouraged to make a pilgrimage to Los Angeles, such as Frank Lloyd Wright, Richard Neutra, and Rudolf Schindler, have now been augmented with a human equivalent, an exponent that now prompts architects to turn inward. Moss is alone in instinctively recognizing this profound change and in seeking to represent it in his work. Pittard Sullivan is the ultimate example of this.

Eric Owen Moss: Green Umbrella
The number of ribs in the original concept was
eventually reduced.

Moss's overt recognition of the cataclysmic aspect of the
city's history and essential character is a clue of recognition of
the wider agenda to which architecture answers in Los Angeles.
The towers in the northern side of Rhino Records, or R1 – which
replaced the sloping roof of the earlier design to boost the
square footage to a level that would be acceptable to the new
client – have been joined by a playful series of pneumatic stairs
that scissor between them. The angles of the stairs, based on the
preliminary sketches by Moss, have been generated from folding
diagrams, but he also mentions the mountains in the distance and
it is tempting to make an analogy between the shifting of tectonic
plates that causes the earthquakes that are so prevalent in the
region and the tectonics of this particular segment of the design.
A building with moving parts has been an unattainable goal of
many architects, such as Richard Rogers and Renzo Piano in the
Pompidou Center in Paris, which they originally intended to have
rise and fall on its huge columns like the rear end of a Renault,
but Moss had been one of the few to realize the goal at Rhino
Records, with its movable stairs.

Pittard Sullivan has been planned to incorporate a second
phase of expansion, a bridge that will spring from the tilted box
and conical lobby piece across the parking lot on the southern
side. Moss describes it as "growing off the lobby, which is the
fundamental organizational piece in the building – and stretching
into the next site or piece of property, which the owner has
purchased. But the bridge has a very different strategy for
making itself. It actually goes from vertically acknowledging the
elevator core that splits the lobby to transform into what is
essentially a horizontal building. It has its own order, strategy and
ideas." Box-like structures, which straddle the traffic islands in
the parking lot, serve as the piers of the span and it is the
circulation feeder for them. The bridge has an elegant, blade-like
profile in section, finally providing the tangible piece of the Pittard
Sullivan puzzle with regard to the parking lot: that the building
was generated by, and defends itself from, a long wall and spiky
trusses. This is another convincing instance of the "connected," or
"conjunctive" points strategy that Eric Moss and Frederick Smith
are carrying out. No building in the Hayden Tract is being dealt
with as an entity and each is seen as part of an interrelated urban
chess game that the developer and architect have redesigned.

Eric Owen Moss: Green Umbrella, Los Angeles
Conceptual drawings show the architect's intention to use
existing bow-string trusses in an upside-down, radial pattern –
resembling an inverted umbrella – as a roof.

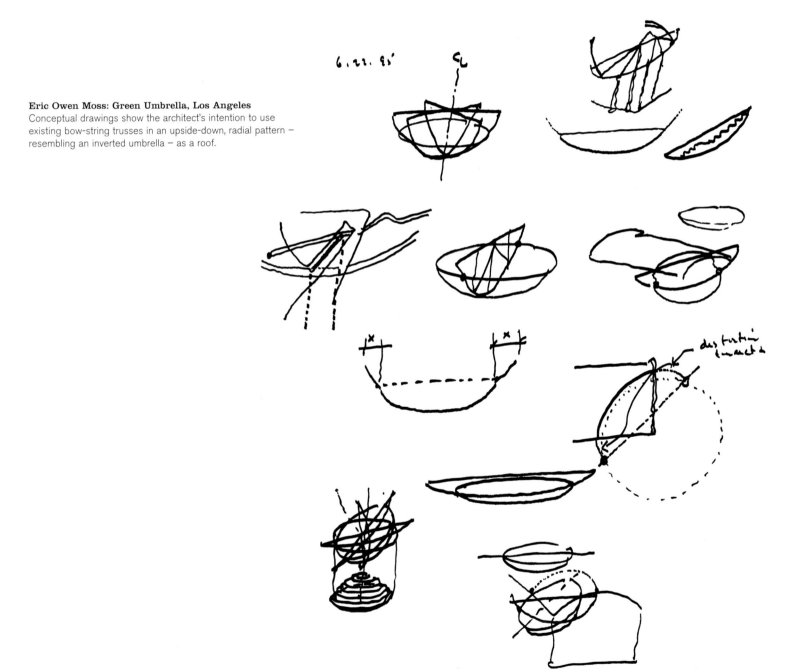

Eric Owen Moss: Green Umbrella
Extensive diagramming was used to develop the final
configuration of the glass roof.

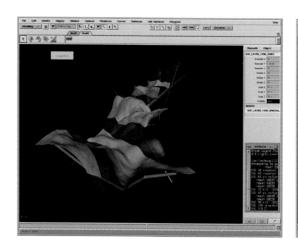

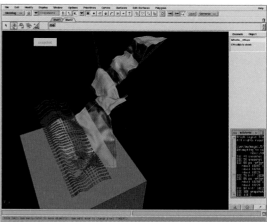

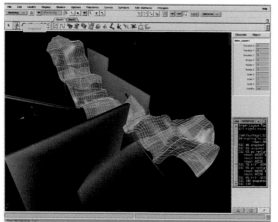

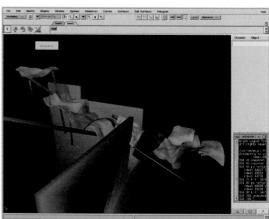

Eric Owen Moss: Green Umbrella
In spite of painstaking studies and preparation, some pieces of the glass roof had to be hand formed while still hot in the autoclave, to avoid breakage.

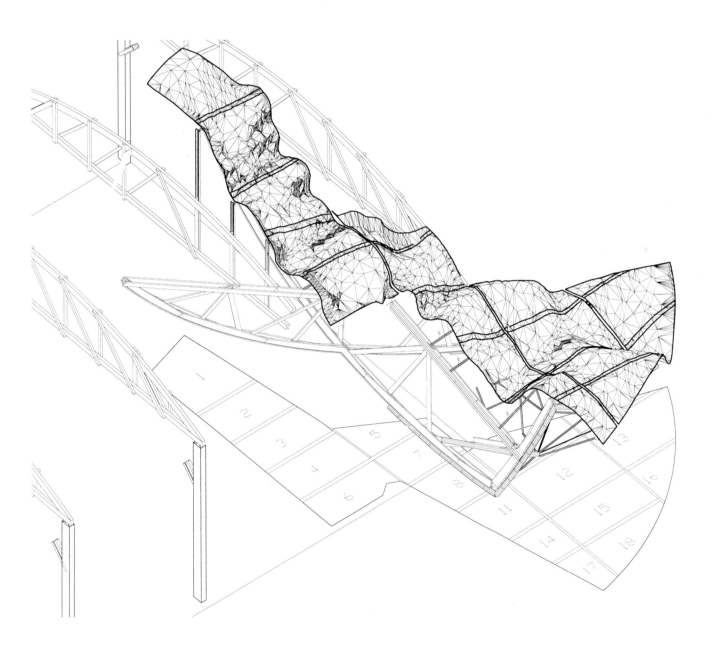

Eric Owen Moss: Green Umbrella
In their final installation, the ribs of the trusses
are set off against the lava-like flow of glass.

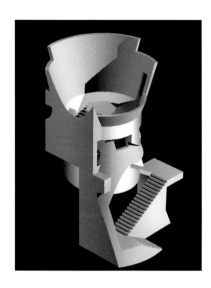

Eric Owen Moss: Samitaur, Los Angeles
Complex spatial and formal relationships are more quickly
studied by computer.

Green Umbrella

The remnants of the bow trusses – which project at various
lengths through the wall that Moss describes as the crucial line
of demarcation between the realm of the automobile, the parking
lot, and the intentionally dark internal world of digital enterprise –
are not unique to Pittard Sullivan. More specifically, bow-string
trusses are reused wherever they occur in Moss's reinventions
of Culver City factories and warehouses in ways that explain his
new concept for the building. In the so-called Green Umbrella
project, for example, to offset possible cities-within psychosis the
existing trusses were sardonically reconfigured as spokes
radiating out from a central shaft, and as at Pittard Sullivan they
are equally expressive of Moss's intentions. The paradoxical
juxtaposition of inside and outside that is obvious in other
instances, such as the Gary Group, where a similar juxtaposition
with a parking lot exists, is drawn out in Pittard Sullivan's south-
facing phalanx, where the skeleton of the building literally
protrudes through its skin. If seen another way, the skin seems to
be pushed inward by the toughness of the external environment
– the asphalt field and steel wall of cars opposing it – and this
is the serious play in which the architect is and always has been
engaged. The wrapper, or skin, of the building becomes more
than an enclosing surface, it is used as an opportunity for
commentary on the nature of architecture itself.

Eric Moss, as sculptor-architect, has proven he has a
remarkably well developed three-dimensional sense, but as the
images of his work in these pages show, this has now been
augmented with the latest computer technology, making his
spatial reach and power of visualization even more formidable.
The Green Umbrella performance hall confirms the close
relationship between digital technology and individual intuition
now in play in the Moss office, and offers an important
counterpoint to Frank Gehry's belief that computerized control
will re-establish the architect's historic role as leader of the
construction process. The glass canopy of the Green Umbrella,
which cascades over the seating like a crystal waterfall, tested
the limits of such control due to unpredictable variables in the
material. Steel forms for the grillage that contours the molten
glass were able to be precisely cut by computer, but even though
all of the angles of this three-dimensional map were theoretically
correct, the glass shattered when it cooled. An "S" clip intended
to secure and seal the overlapping edges was also difficult to
implement because parallel lines were impossible to maintain,
forcing readjustment of the detail. Moss tells an amusing, but
highly significant, story of finally forming the glass manually while
it was still hot to get the folds he wanted without having it break.
His conclusion is that while computer fabrication methods are
very precise and controlled up to a point, there are some
instances that require empirical intervention.

Eric Owen Moss: Samitaur
As with most projects in "Conjunctive Points," another iteration –
the shell-shaped structure on the left of the existing building –
is planned for Samitaur in the future.

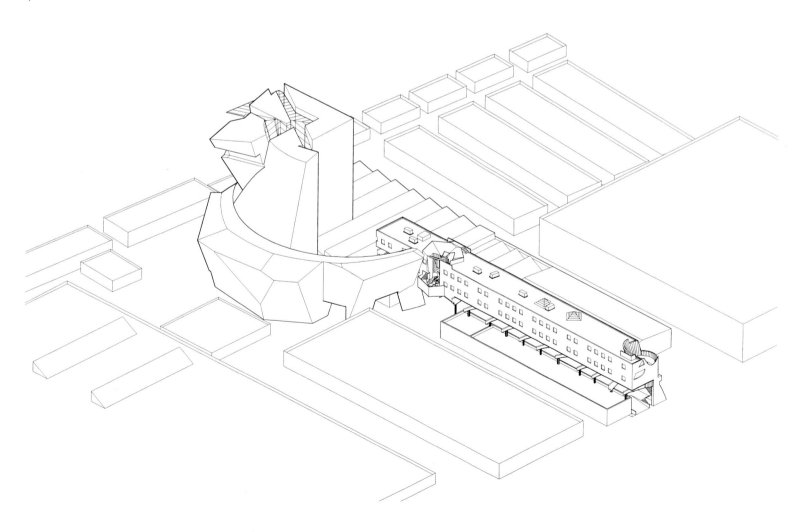

Eric Owen Moss: Samitaur
This balcony, at the center of the linear building, opens out to a parking lot.

Eric Owen Moss: Samitaur
To emphasize the gritty social reality around it, Moss has intentionally positioned the overlooks in Samitaur to face typical urban scenery.

Eric Owen Moss: Samitaur
Signature entrances such as this one are also art in the service of economics, serving as corporate advertising.

Eric Owen Moss: Samitaur
Section showing the pyramidal roof vents in
the center of the building.

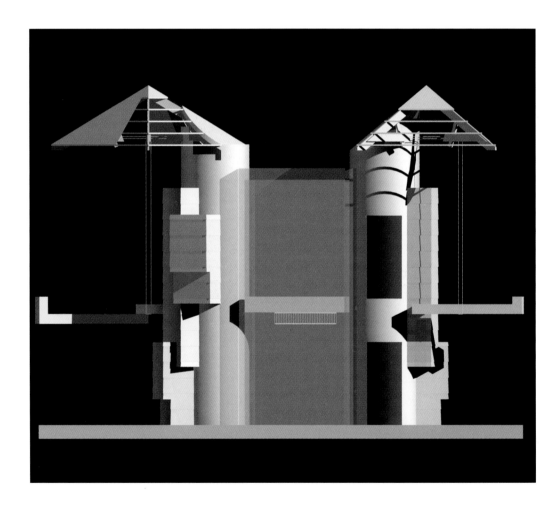

Eric Owen Moss: Samitaur

Seeking to offer typologies appropriate to Los Angeles, Moss has used Samitaur as a prototype for how to take advantage of unused space over freeways.

Eric Owen Moss: Samitaur

Soil conditions and bearing capacity determined the location of columns and frames, which all differ.

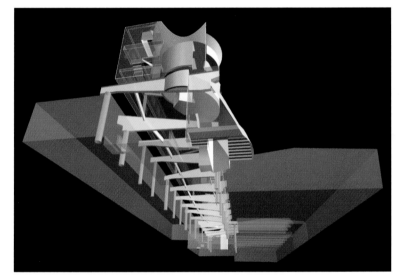

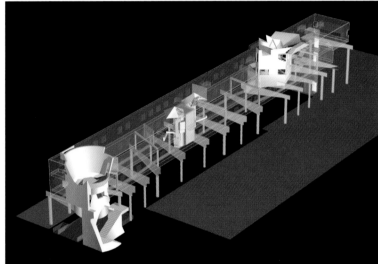

Eric Owen Moss: Samitaur
The smooth, gray, troweled surface of Samitaur contrasts with
the brick of a commercial unit below.

The form of the glass waterfall was driven by acoustical as well as purely aesthetic considerations; the relatively small performance hall it covers was conceived as an elevated, suspended theater in the round, with some of the audience viewing center stage from ground level, slightly below it. A large garage, as part of the Green Umbrella-Stealth group, will accommodate the cars that now occupy the space where this part of the audience is intended to be seated, so that this lynchpin of Moss's and developers Frederick and Laurie Smith's strategy to imbue Conjunctive Points with cultural facilities can finally work as intended.

In spite of Moss's enthusiastic embrace of computer technology because of the possibilities it offers to enhance his considerable perceptual skills, graphic exploration still plays an important part in his designs, as is indicated by the hybrid collages of images in both media that are often part of the office's presentations. Freehand sketches of the glass roof of the Green Umbrella complement digital precision in a reflexive way, without either one predominating.

Samitaur

The Samitaur project is the model that both Smith and Moss have invoked as being the closest relative of Pittard Sullivan, or its more extroverted alter ego, and it helps to clarify Samitaur's agenda through comparison. If Pittard Sullivan presents an internalized parking lot topology, Samitaur, which takes Laurie Smith's middle name, proposes a solution for the freeway. An existing right of way on the site required an ingenious and necessarily expensive system of columns and girders that dance in a row under the linear structure, answering to ground conditions below. "The block has a 48-foot [15-meter] height limit," Moss explains, "and the width is limited by fire department regulations. Underneath the block there's a required clearance of 15 feet [4.5 meters] for trucks. So Samitaur is the block, the limits of the block, the cutting out of the block, but never adding to the block." Like Pittard Sullivan, Samitaur also has been designed to accept a second phase, described as more "covert" than the highly visible bridge in the air that precedes it. This addition continues the horizontal line of the building, rather than being perpendicular to it (as planned for Pittard Sullivan), but it does also spring from one of the major episodic events of an otherwise linear scheme.

At Pittard Sullivan, the lobby is a singular episode, but Samitaur has two sculptural pieces that interrupt the otherwise systematic structure. These episodes are strategically placed and flip, or reverse, on the plan. One celebrates the main function of this particular invented topology, a gateway on the west side of the bar, toward the rear of the site that marks the exit point for trucks using the access right of way. When design began in 1989, two lines of one-story brick-faced spaces, intended for industrial use, were placed on either side of the covered roadway, with the enormous piers that hold up the linear block above woven through them. These spaces do not connect with the upper block, but are self-sufficient, with their own roof. This pentagonal bite into the side of the long rectangular block has a stairway servicing the three floors of offices, which is set inside this open court, as well as a balcony skewed for a northern, mountain view. The floor of the balcony has a shallow pool with a steel mesh footbridge over it, leading to a narrow deck adjacent to the railing, the analogies recalling a similar combination at the Barnsdall house by Frank Lloyd Wright, where water around a fireplace illuminated by a skylight recalls the four elements of earth, air, fire, and water.

The second sculptural episode, or as Moss calls it, the "idiosyncratic incident within a repetitive matrix," is the even more spectacular main entrance to the Samitaur complex at the southeast corner, which establishes the image of the building for the public because it faces the access road and parking lot across from it. The conical geometry that has been used in the Pittard Sullivan lobby emerges again here, stripped of its outer layer, looking like a large chess piece on the game board that Smith and Moss now control. The larger significance of Samitaur, however, is that it is just off the edge of that board, over the Culver City border into an "economically challenged" sector of Los Angeles that is close to the flashpoint of the 1992 riots. Frederick Smith found the riots to be both disturbing and motivating, and feels that they "made it clear that something basic was missing in our city that had never been addressed by our endless system of social welfare programs. After the riots, as a personal protest against how they were being analyzed in the national and international press, I decided to formulate my own plan for social welfare. I decided that I would implement it right where the riots had occurred, believing that if I could create a job-based urban development in a depressed and violence-ridden area, 'garden-variety' apartments would naturally follow."

The broader significance of these buildings, as part of the "conjunctive points" chain that the developer and architect have been deliberately forging, relates to permanence. Do they have enduring value in the conventional sense of Louis Kahn's search for a "timeless architecture," as realized in the Salk Institute at La Jolla, California, for example? Kahn sought inspiration in historical and primarily Roman examples, as well as in the materiality that made those examples durable. He began his search with brick, considered questionable in the canon of the Modern Movement because of its traditional associations, and evolved it into a personal language with classical roots that was very articulate. He wanted his buildings to last a long time and hoped that, when they had outlived their usefulness, they would become romantic ruins. Projected usefulness at the time Kahn was designing was 50 years at the most, with few buildings ever reaching that age before major renovation or demolition. The increasing integration between architecture and the consumer cycle, or commercialism, has further abbreviated that short life cycle, and architects can hardly expect either the 100 or more years of use that was taken for granted at the beginning of the twentieth century, or the half-life of that expectation that Kahn hoped to ensure. Eric Moss is realistic and relatively free of the self-delusion that many architects continue to perpetuate as part of the myth of creative individuality that continues to thrive in the profession. While he has actively perpetuated the myth of the single creative source, he understands the spirit and impersonal demands of the consumer cycle, as well as the commercial outlook of his patron. Frederick Smith is an enlightened developer, but an astute businessman, nonetheless. The Pittard Sullivan lobby, Green Umbrella corner, and Samitaur public entrance are habitable sculpture, but are also good business because they attract attention, cause controversy, and confer status on the client who leases space in the buildings to which they are attached. The not-so-secret tactic that the developer and architect use is to ensure that these *tours de force* do not compromise leasable area.

Moore, Ruble, Yudell: Yorkin House, Los Angeles
Simulations of environmental conditions contributed to the
final layout of this beach house.

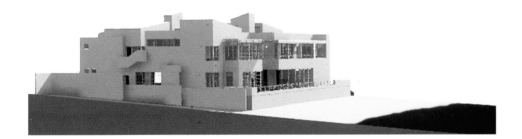

Moore, Ruble, Yudell: Bursa Vludag Ski Resort, Turkey
A remarkable approximation of winter conditions in Bursa was
achieved in this rendering.

Taken together, Moss's instincts about Pittard Sullivan, the Green Umbrella, and Samitaur are hard to fault. He challenges convention where he believes he has a good chance of winning, testing the limits of our standard notions of where the line of demarcation between inside and outside should be, what the wrapper should be built of, what it should look like, and how long it should last. More importantly, he also tests the usual notions of what the urban topologies of the future should be, demanding that city planners take notice of the reality check he is proposing. Frederick Smith's courage in crossing the line from Pittard Sullivan in Culver City to Samitaur in South Central has gained the team of developer and architect the respect and support of the planning establishment and, as is usually the case, the move was not entirely altruistic. The result has been a discussion with city authorities about making "conjunctive points" an "architecturally free zone," exempt from a majority of the zoning and height restrictions that usually apply, without compromising on life safety issues.

Whether it is finally established or not, the fact that it is being discussed at all by the planning establishment is an indication of the serious contribution that Smith and Moss are making to the contemporary urban debate. The position they are trying to advance is critical, involving a thorough reexamination of planning approaches. Their effort marks the first time that a convincing range of alternatives have been put forward as models for constructive change in ways that do not threaten business as usual. As one of those models, Pittard Sullivan deserves close examination, and the hybrid that appears under the microscope must be accepted on its own terms.

Moore, Ruble, Yudell's Hybrid Approach

At the opposite end of the theoretical spectrum – and the city – from Eric Moss, Moore, Ruble, Yudell bring Michael Kwartler's idea of a "kit of parts" (see pp.45–51) around full circle in their response to a challenge by a prominent design magazine to design a protypical house for the new millennium. Seeking to balance their concern for basic human needs with rapid changes in demographics, technology, the environment, and the workplace, Moore, Ruble, Yudell approached the problem as the design of a process "articulated through the combination of freehand drawing and digital imaging." They used this hybrid technique to create a vocabulary of building components that can be assembled in different ways depending on the client brief and site conditions. They then digitally simulated the qualities of light and space for each of the most obvious configurations and adaptations to the lifetime of changing family patterns that might take place in the houses.

The kit of parts includes the five elements listed here. "Heavy elements," such as thick walls and hearths, help to satisfy the basic needs for a sense of protection, shelter, and connection to the land. "Light elements," for example trellises, sun shades, sliding walls, and screens, allow for flexible change of room use and degree of openness and closure relative to the environment. Light-weight screens and metal vents can use evolving solar technology. "Support elements" include plumbing and kitchen cores, wind scoops, light wells, solar and wind collectors, and technology links that change with time and need. "Interior elements" are each flexible enough to accommodate a range of uses. Rooms provide for different kinds of activities and moods. Examples include a "great room" for living and entertaining, an "intimate room" for reading and meditation, a "loft room" for work and home projects, and a "wet room" for bathing. "Landscape rooms" are an array of different exterior spaces including open bridges, courtyards, and terraces that extend the sense of interior living to exterior spaces. Activities that take place outside include dining, entertaining, work, and recreation. Multiple exterior rooms are configured throughout both house plans.

To test the kit, the architects chose two sites typical of Southern California: a flat 50-by-150-foot (15-by-45-meter) urban plot and another in the suburbs on a sloping quarter-acre plot. The urban site lent itself to a linear organization along a central horizontal gallery, with rooms opening up on either side, alternating with small outdoor courtyards, terraces, and roof gardens. The guiding principle was to allow as many rooms as possible to have three exposures. The suburban site, on the other hand, allowed division into two clusters, connected by an open-air bridge, with a two-car garage and home office included in the segment closest to the street. The home office is added in hopeful anticipation of the increase in time spent at home that electronic technology has long been expected to bring about – as the obvious antithesis of Eric Moss's efforts to provide a humane alternative to the international tendency toward digital mosh pits.

Such standardization by MRY is a definite shift in direction from their single-family detached homes that remain one staple of their portfolio, such as the Shmuger-Hamagami house in Pacific Palisades and the Yorkin House in Malibu, but the digital graphic hybrid method is beginning to be used on these as well. It has also been helpful in maintaining the traditional grounding the firm seeks, while providing the more systematized approach required by larger projects, such as several housing complexes and a ski resort completed in Turkey in 1999. The Miramar Villas in Guzelce and the Nautilus Condominiums in Yesilyurt, both for Emta A.S., were digitally modeled in the Santa Monica office, in tandem with graphic overlays. The ski resort in Bursa Vludag, for Arslan A.S., was modeled in the office of the local associate architect, Talu Limited, with digital teleconferencing used to help coordinate ideas.

An even more dramatic example of graphic digital hybrid is a competition design for the Sun Law Power Station in Los Angeles, which was a creative collaboration between client and architect, once the commission was secured. Graphic sketches were scanned in and worked on in Form-Z to make this possible.

Keep the Lead In

Those who predict the demise of the pencil, or who gleefully proclaim it has already gone the way of the buggy whip and typewriter, should consider the extent to which many practitioners are now effectively integrating graphic and digital techniques across a broad spectrum of applications, as indicated by Eric Owen Moss and Moore, Ruble, Yudell, among a myriad of other firms that could be mentioned. Whether used at the conceptual stage, as it is by Gehry (see pp.122–33) and Moss, or as a symbolic statement of the architect's traditional association with graphics, as with MRY, or as a reality check on virtual space at various stages in the digital process, as in the example of Jon Jerde (see pp.147–9), it seems the pencil may still be around for some time to come.

Moore, Ruble, Yudell: Sun Law Power Station
The new power plant is located in a mixed residential-industrial neighborhood called South Gate in Los Angeles.

Moore, Ruble, Yudell: Sun Law Power Station
This sequence of studies shows how MRY has been mixing media to more effectively describe their ideas to their client.

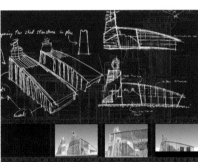

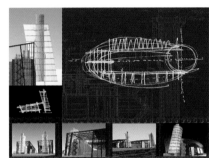

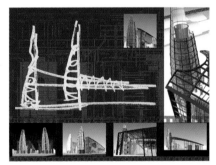

Moore, Ruble, Yudell: Sun Law Power Station
Sun Law Energy Corporation specializes in converting natural gas
to electricity using clean energy sources.

Moore, Ruble, Yudell: Sun Law Power Station
Designers draw on computer printouts, and then scan the new hybrid images to "corrupt the media."

Moore, Ruble, Yudell: Sun Law Power Station
MRY did an extensive study of towers – as lighthouses, energy sources, markers, and cultural symbols.

Moore, Ruble, Yudell: Sun Law Power Station
To unify the various parts of the plant, the elliptical towers were juxtaposed against the sweeping arc of steel canopies, with the two units slightly staggered to provide a recognizable silhouette from the 710 freeway.

chapter 5
a time of transition:
the computer in education

206

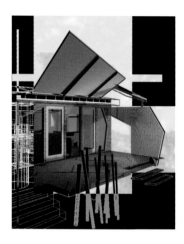

Yuwen Peng: Sunset house
Young architects starting their own firms are directed by their
educational and apprenticeship experience.

A TIME OF TRANSITION: THE COMPUTER IN EDUCATION

The application of computer education in schools of architecture
mirrors that of the profession, with the same range of emphasis
from using it as a tool to making it integral to the design process
that has just been described in previous chapters. Students
leaving school during the first decade of the twenty-first century
are the final cadre of a transitional generation; when that
transition is complete practice will have irrevocably changed,
becoming the culmination of the process that is so dramatically
underway. In the United States alone, it is estimated that because
of the economic prosperity that has largely been the result of
the media and information revolution, 98 percent of the class of
2000 will enter the profession at an average annual income of
$28,000. While this starting salary has not significantly changed
over the last 20 years, their enhanced technical skills, compared
to the older principals, project managers, and architects who are
less proficient in the use of computers, will make advancement
easier, allowing them to reach $43,000 a year within three years.
During that experience, nearly 70 percent of their time will be
spent in front of a monitor, and while this is arguably the same
duration as drafting in the past, there is a significant difference
that directly affects the responsibility of educators in the near
future. Surveys of computer use in offices worldwide are
inadequate, but one carried out in the mid-1990s in the United
States involving a stratified random sample size of 450, showed

that interns are much more proficient in the most commonplace
software – Computer-Aided Drafting and Design (CADD) and
AutoCAD – than the older architects, project managers, and
principals who are expected to train them in what is still assumed
to be a mentor-apprentice relationship.[77]

Where Have All the Mentors Gone?

This proficiency gap has several important implications, the first
of which is that the passing on of practical knowledge – the
real world component of a young professional's education that
is often missing in academic experience – has been disrupted,
placing the responsibility on the intern to find answers to
questions about building systems, detailing, and procedural
matters that were once provided by experienced colleagues.
In the United States at least, which has not adopted the
European custom of a study year spent gaining experience in
an office, this shift fundamentally changes the tacit agreement
that has existed between the schools, where the emphasis is
on the theoretical aspects of design, and the office, which has
been expected to fill in the prodigious gaps in graduates'
knowledge. In spite of the consistent complaints registered on
American Institute of Architects surveys, that schools do not
adequately prepare students to be effective in the office, this tacit
arrangement has been upheld, perhaps because those with
experience have felt it was their duty to support and perpetuate
a system that had made their own professional development

Yuwen Peng: Sunset house
Even the most modest commissions, like this small house,
are now realized using digital technology.

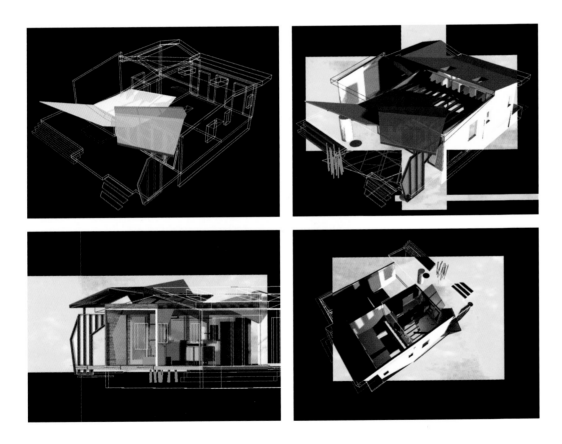

John Weidner: Studio exercise
Rotation of the three-dimensional image assures that nothing is left to chance.

John Weidner: Studio exercise
In this studio exercise conducted by Mayne, elements were examined in the same way materials were studied in the famous basic design course once given at the Bauhaus.

Bennett Shen and Kim Groves: Copenhagen project
As always, instructors emphasize their own value systems in the design studio, and in Thom Mayne's case, this now includes a strong belief in the importance of digital imaging, evident in this student project.

John Weidner: Studio exercise
The computer now offers students the ability to microscopically
examine each detail.

possible. But now, with interns increasingly relegated to repetitive
computing, isolated outside the learning loop because of dexterity
and a special skill that is the cyber-equivalent of being assigned
to the model shop, this arrangement must change. Inspiring
alternatives already exist, such as the Dublin Institute of
Technology, where the curriculum includes a mandatory year of
learning construction techniques in a parallel facility. American
universities have rejected such instruction on the grounds that it
would reduce them to the status of a trade school, the implication
being that learning construction would somehow compromise
theoretical idealism. The example of Howard Roark in Ayn Rand's
The Fountainhead still touches a nerve: the alternative of hard
labour in the quarry should only be considered if all other
possibilities for creative expression are thwarted.

Somewhere along the line, the Bauhaus principle of
integrating the ideals of design theory, which Roark represents,
with the production he was forced to subsist on was bifurcated.
The Gothic paragon of divinely inspired communal cooperation –
subsequently filtered through Arts and Crafts sensibilities that
were transformed into an early modern, secular ideology – was
lost when transplanted in the United States. Coinciding with the
rapid, post-war growth of the media, the image of modernism
was easily and, as it turns out, too superficially adopted,
while the ideology, especially as related to making, was lost.
With the increasing emphasis on digital skill, yet another layer
of abstraction by simulacra has been introduced, with the
potential of separating students even further from the reality
of construction.

The Digital Marriage of Design and Production

The exhilarating counterpoint to this increasing distance from material reality is the position championed by Frank Gehry and best demonstrated in the Guggenheim Museum in Bilbao (see pp.127–33), in which CATIA has been shown to allow a close integration between design and construction. Gehry believes that the facility of the computer to convert documented details into built form simply through the transfer of a disk will return the architect, as the locus of information, to center stage in the construction process. This assumes, of course, that the details are correct in the first place. It is knowledgeability, not technique, that will earn the respect of contractors and clients. What impressed Gehry, and finally sold him on computer use, was that it would allow him to build forms that he would previously not have considered because contractors wouldn't touch them; it reassured them and freed his imagination. But, like Picasso knowing anatomy before being able to convincingly fragment it, Gehry had long experience in putting a functionally operational, structurally stable, leakproof building together before his digital flights of fancy began, and that hard-won knowledge has informed his art. Students and interns must now reach that point with less experienced guidance.

Meanwhile, a general observation, not yet substantiated by methodical research, is that in the absence of a fully developed pedagogy and open debate on the issues raised here, the student's lot is subject to individual interest and motivation as well as the inclination and skill of his or her dean and studio instructor. Very few schools seem to have an integrated plan for introducing computers into all studios, focusing on a selection of courses that teach proficiency instead. The idea of computer theory is still a completely alien notion, due in part to a feeling of technological inevitability that precludes discussion, as well as to curricular triage, which addresses the skills graduates need to get jobs, complete internships, and pass registration examinations, before less "pragmatic" issues can be raised. Where universities used to be evaluated by prospective students according to their design direction, they are now increasingly considered according to the number of computer gurus present and how cutting-edge they are, and letting the computer lead is favored over using it as a tool. There is no question that, in spite of the direction preferred by any individual dean, director, or tutor, the student's life is now made much easier by the computer in many respects. Set-up time is long and laborious on orthogonal projects, but once a plan is established sections, perspectives, elevations, walk-throughs, and animations are exponentially faster, providing a much clearer understanding of three-dimensional spatial relationships than conventional, graphic techniques allowed.

My Woo: Study exercise under Thom Mayne
The biological aspects of physical structure become
more evident at a microscopic scale.

My Woo: Study exercise under Thom Mayne
The adage that an entire building can be contained in a detail
now seems much more relevant to students.

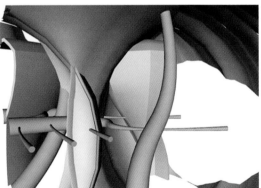

Franco Wu Fang at USC: Chinatown project
Structural framing can now be studied as an integral
part of form.

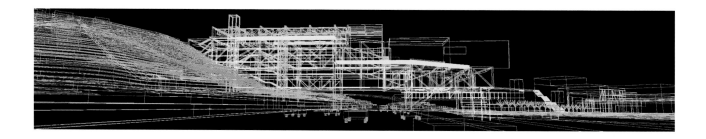

Elevations, which were once difficult for students to
visualize, are now much easier to construct.

The area above freeways and surface streets is not efficiently used in Los Angeles, a situation this study aims to change.

This project utilizes a 20-foot (6-meter) drop in the site contours as a way of creating a gateway to Chinatown in Los Angeles.

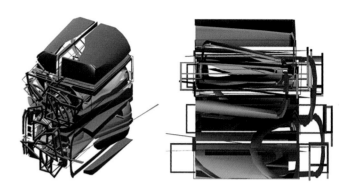

Robin Sambo: Student project under Thom Mayne
The mechanistic aspect of much student work today
begins at the micro scale.

Computer design technology has also opened up unexpected possibilities for teachers, such as one history lecture, developed by Robert Timme, dean of the School of Architecture at the University of Southern California, demonstrates. As Timme explains:

> Before the computer, design concepts and processes were difficult to present. By combining various software programs complex topics can be shown in a visual format that is clear, descriptive, and animated. This lecture, Order and Design, is a presentation of a system of three-dimensional architectonic components and the fundamental way they can be ordered to achieve spatial definition and hierarchy. The presentation utilizes well known buildings as examples of various organizational strategies. It moves through a design process, illustrating the development of a simple concept.

The initial set of images depicts columns that are seen with different spacing. This idea of intercolumnation was essential to the development of the Greek and Roman temple. The presentation of various spacing in simple elevation would not convey an understanding of the importance of this concept. Showing the columns obliquely and in three dimensions illustrates the view from where the altar would have been as in the Parthenon. This series of images facilitates a discussion of issues ranging from phenomenal transparency to the rituals and processional sequences related to the temples. The three-dimensional images and diagrams were created with Form-Z and Photoshop and presented in PowerPoint.

Animation and walk-through visualization also make students more aware of structural hierarchies in their own projects; the implacably logical elevation of columns and walls rigorously demonstrates the implications of two-dimensional design decisions and partially solves the chronic problem of integrating structure into the design studio. Paperless PowerPoint presentations are generally more organized and self-explanatory, making more cogent responses possible.

CADD Caveats

CADD has had limitations, however. Developed in the mid-1960s, it first became available to architects in 1970, but for the next decade, only large firms could afford a seat, operated by a specially trained technician and costing the equivalent of US$ 100,000, and deal with the proprietary purchase of hardware, software, and maintenance contracts. The appearance of the personal computer in 1982 broke the market open and made competing software available, but CADD and AutoCAD continued to dominate, and until relatively recently their main emphasis was production documentation, rather than design.[78]

As recently as the mid-1990s, an investigation into the connection between CADD use and design philosophy in America concluded that computer systems have auspiciously arrived just in time to solve design problems that have become

Robin Sambo
The computer has x-ray vision that allows the juxtaposition of many layers at once.

too complex to be dealt with by conventional methods, but that "the use of the computer for design is not as successful or widespread as for drafting and documentation." At the time of this survey, which involved a significant number of firms, it was estimated that slightly fewer than 14 percent used CADD for design and that "some CADD packages appear to support design needs better while others support documentation needs better… this inadequacy could be one reason, as researchers have noted, that the integration of computing into the design process has been minimal." [79]

The relative orthogonal rigidity of CADD, which has led to the insightful criticism by Alberto Pérez-Gomez that it represents the scientific continuity of modernistic rationality, is legible in built form. [80] Michael Benedict, who in 1991 edited *Cyberspace: First Steps*, one of the first attempts to understand the computer phenomenon in architecture, has related his impression that "because of the way AutoCAD works, I can always tell when I walk into a space designed using it. It is built up in layers of plans, not in sections or models." [81]

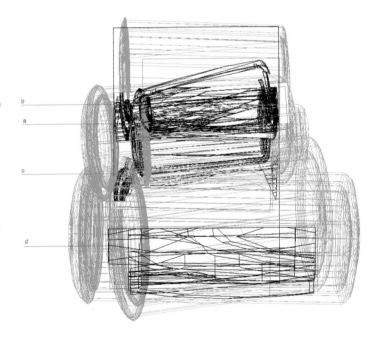

Melanie Beisswenger at USC: Student project
Beisswenger used Lebbeus Woods's book *Houses in Tension/ Reconstruction of the Air-Space* as the inspiration for this animated project.

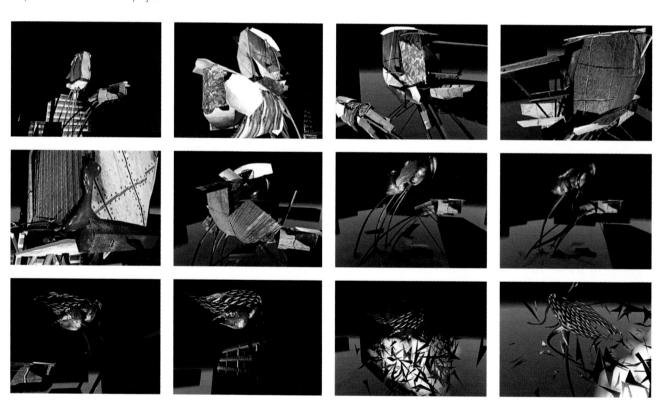

Melanie Beisswenger at USC: Student project
Beisswenger modeled, rendered, and animated this
form in 3D StudioMAX. Premiere was used to
construct the final movie.

The New Wave(front) Alias: Tsunami

Releases 13 and 14 of AutoCAD and 3D Studio Max have
made more design-friendly modeling possible, but it has taken
new software, such as Silicon Graphics' Alias Wavefront with its
animation capacity, as well as a growing interest in manipulating
complex algorithms to finally transform the computer into a
powerful, creative force. The names of a new breed of cybernaut,
such as Karl S. Chu, Lars Spuybroek of NOX, Greg Lynn, ECOi,
Oosterhius Associates, UN Studio, and Stephen Perrella seem
to be popping up like mushrooms after a rainstorm, the first crest
of what appears to be a tsunami of paradigmatic change to come.

With the notable exception of prophets John Frazer at the
Architectural Association in London, William Mitchell at MIT, or
Bernard Tschumi at Columbia, among a few others, most schools
seem pedagogically unprepared to deal with this shift and in
the meantime, students are left to fend for themselves. Under
pressure, they seem willing to trade speed for creativity, or even
worse, confuse the two. The sense of empowerment that such
speed offers also seems to make it difficult for them to edit.
More is better, and the quality of space is frequently sacrificed to

Keith Ireland at USC: Student project
This prototype for a studio of the future incorporates a mega-sound stage production bungalow, including a television sound stage, a working studio, and technical support.

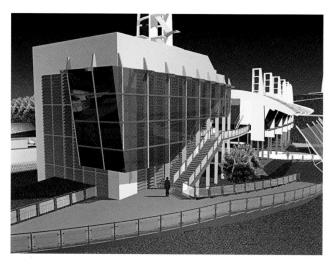
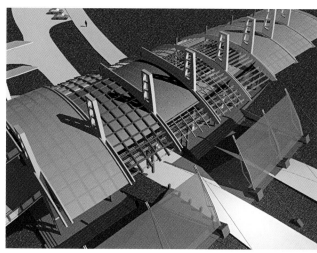

Keith Ireland at USC: Student project
Top: Repetitive units seem to appear more often in student
projects because of the relative ease in generating them.

Bottom: Sections were once problematic for students, but
are now more a case of giving the computer the right
instructions, within the limits of a given program.

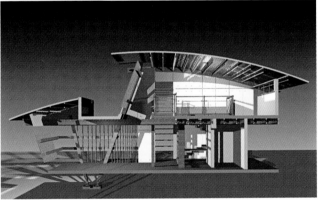

the overwhelming temptation to "repeat." But then, space has
now also taken on a different meaning; since it is only virtual it is
losing a grounding in reality. All of the impressive strides made
by social philosophers, such as Henri Lefevbre and Michel
Foucault, especially in relation to cultural differentiation and
gendered space, are disregarded by the latest algorithmic
transformations, as is environmental context. The groundswell of
interest in sustainability – which shows no signs of abating after
first being defined by the Brundtland Commission in the late
1980s and then of the Agenda 21 Conference in Rio de Janeiro
in the 1990s – has percolated into architectural curricula, and can
be traced to the same imperative to discover the structure of
difference that drives the growing philosophy of architectural
space. But it is increasingly antithetical to what is happening, or
is likely to happen soon, in many studios, which is worrying.

Yokoi Satoko at USC: Millennium project
USC faculty members Karen Kensek and Doug Noble
posted these proposals on the Internet, and they were
reviewed by faculty from universities around the world.

Madhu Gupta at USC: Historical study
A more detailed study of the structures of historical
precedents is an added advantage of computer imaging.

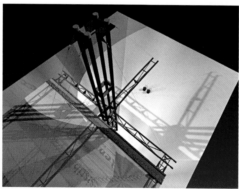

Chris Stage at USC: Sant'Elia project
This sequence shows an interpretation of the inspiration
behind the visionary schemes of Futurist architect
Antonio Sant'Elia.

Stacey Lin at USC: Student project
Thanks to computer programs, site plans can now be
rendered in perspective.

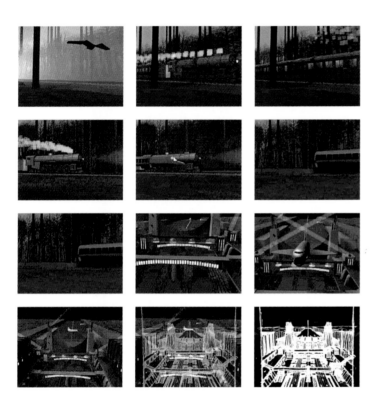

Datascape versus Gaia

Many would vehemently protest that the process oriented
programmes being individually developed to transform contextual
information into "datascapes," often overlayered with formal
historical palimpsests, do reconnect virtual design to the real
natural world. The fallacy in this argument, however, is that pure
information can never really convey meaning in an adequate way,
that Dreyfus' point, about human intuition being necessary to
guide cybernetic overload, is now more valid than ever. What is
certain, however, as the next generations head into the future,
is that talent seems to continue to rise to the top, no matter what
medium of expression is used.

224

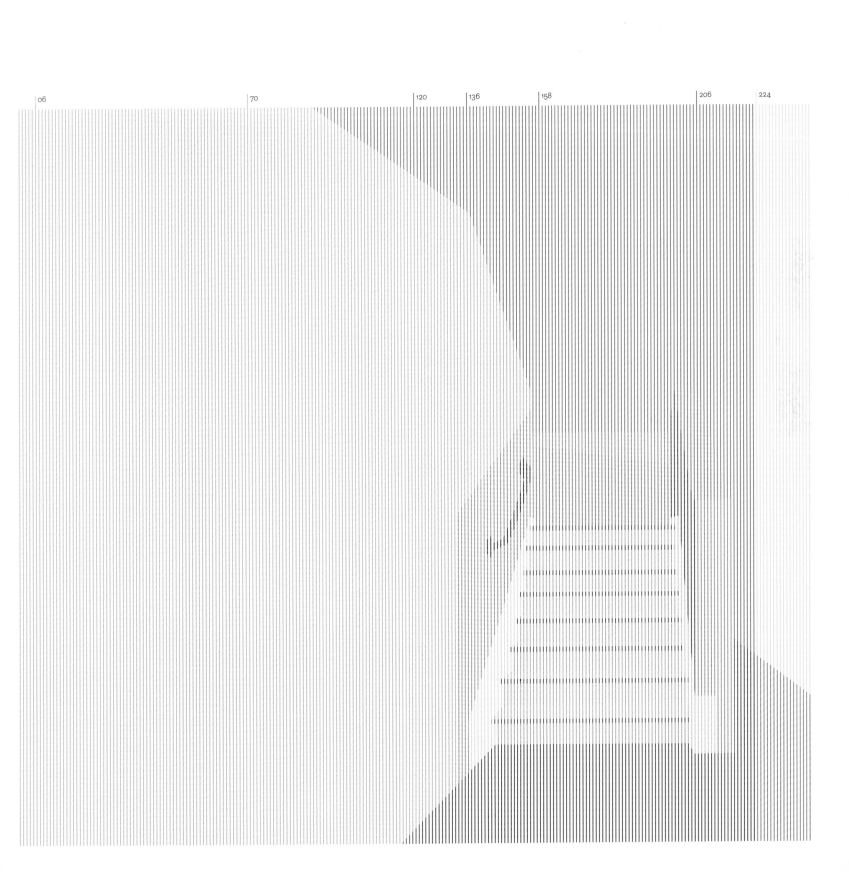

endnotes

Introduction

1   Frank Rich: "The Future Will Resume in 15 Days," *New York Times* (Dec. 8, 1999), p. A31

2   Langdon Winner: *The Whale and the Reactor: A Search for Limits in an Age of High Technology* (University of Chicago Press, 1986) p. 5

3   Calvin Sims: "Angst at Japan Inc, A Nation Frets Over a String of Technological Accidents," *New York Times* (Dec. 2, 1999), p. 5

4   Lawrence Zuckerman: "Is Complexity Interlinked with Disaster?" *New York Times* (Dec. 11, 1999), p. A21. See also Charles Perrow: *Normal Accidents: Living with High Risk Technologies* (Princeton University Press, 1999)

5   Langdon Winner, *op. cit.,* p. 6: "It is taken for granted… that the only reliable sources for improving the human condition stem from new machines, techniques and chemicals."

6   Merrill Lynch advertisement, *New York Times* (March 16, 1999), p. C30

7   Hubert L. Dreyfus: *What Computers Can't Do: A Critique of Artificial Reason* (Harper and Row, New York, 1972), p. 23

8   Dreyfus records these as two phases. Phase I (1957–62) concerns the Cognitive Simulation initiative on language translation, problem solving, and pattern recognition spearheaded by Anthony Oeffinger's work on mechanical translation, which culminated in a report in 1963 by the National Academy of Sciences Research Council. The report found that after $20 million were spent, languages translation was still hindered by programs. In Phase II (1962–7) cybernetics branched out in three directions: (1) in search for the basic principles and self-organizing systems which lead to intelligent behavior; (2) constructing working models of human behavior; and (3) the pursuit of rules or procedures involved in analogical reasoning, or artificial intelligence. See also: Marvin Minsky "Artificial Intelligence," *Scientific American*, Vol. 215 No.3 (Sept. 1966), pp. 25–7, for a detailed description of this initiative, as well as his book *Semantic Information Processing* (MIT Press, Cambridge, MA, 1969) which puts this period into historical perspective.

9   The biological assumption is best presented by John von Neumann in *Probablistic Logics and the Synthesis of Reliable Organisms from Unreliable Components* (Pergamon Press, New York, 1963), Vol. 5, p. 372, in which he says: "the duties (of the central nervous system) include the interpretation of sensory stimuli, of reports of physical and chemical conditions, the control of motor activities and internal chemical levels, the memory function with its very complicated procedures for the transformation of and the search for information and of course, the continuous relaying of coded orders and of more or less quantitative messages. It is possible to handle all of these processes by digital methods."

10   Most importantly, Dreyfus stresses our ability to use "global context" to reduce ambiguity sufficiently without having to formalize, that is, eliminate ambiguity altogether. "Fringe consciousness" takes cues from this context and imbues them with a variety of meanings which must be made explicit in programming. He refers to our ability to exclude unnecessary information as "ambiguity tolerance."

The essence of the rationalist view, now embodied in computer programs (including those used in architectural design) is that the mind is "defined by its capacity to form *representations* of all domains of activity (and)… representing the fixed, context free features of a *domain* and the principles governing their interaction explains the *domain's* intelligibility." Martin Heidegger asserts that the essence of creativity is our ability to evolve complex sequences of behavior patterns for a short-term purpose without an overall goal or purpose in sight, or for any reason.

11   Arthur C. Clarke: *Profiles of the Future: An Inquiry into the Limits of the Possible* (Holt, Rinehart and Winston, New York, 1984), p. 229

12   Joseph Weizenbaum: *Computer Power and Human Reason: From Judgment to Calculation* (W.H. Freeman and Co., San Francisco, 1976), p. 18. Weizenbaum calls a tool a "functional prosthesis" and an "agent for change."

13   Richard E. Sclove: *Democracy and Technology* (Guilford Press, New York, 1995), p. 17. These technological processes in contemporary society become the equivalent of law because they are socially binding, with their own expressions, norms, and values.

14   Frederic Jamison: *Post Modernism, or the Cultural Logic of Late Capitalism* (Duke University Press, 1985)

15   Michael Heim: "The Erotic Ontology of Cyberspace," in Michael Benedict, ed.: *Cyberspace: First Steps* (MIT Press, Cambridge, MA, 1991), p. 63

16   *Ibid.,* p. 65

17   See Mircea Eliade: *The Sacred and the Profane* (Harper and Row, New York, 1961)

18   See James Steele: *Charles Rennie Mackintosh: Synthesis and Form* (Academy Editions, London, 1993). Mackintosh was singled out by the German government, through the agency of Hermann Muthesius, as one of the best practitioners of "English Free Architecture," and so worthy of emulation in their struggle to compete with and capture British manufacturing global market share. Muthesius, in his book, *The English House*, only recently translated into English by Dennis Sharp, focuses on the house as the crucial test of manufacturing prowess; the things produced for use in it, and their quality, affect an entire society. Muthesius, and through him the ideas of Mackintosh, was central to the debate on design education that followed in Germany just prior to and then after World War I, leading to the establishment of the Deutsche Werkbund and the Bauhaus.

19 Beatriz Colomina

20 Bryan S. Turner: "Periodization and Politics in the Postmodern" in Bryan S. Turner, ed.: *Theories of Modernity and Postmodernity* (Sage Publications, London, 1990), p. 4

21 *Ibid.*, p. 5

22 Daniel Bell: *The Coming of Post Industrial Society* (Basic Books, New York, 1976)

23 Jean-François Lyotard: "The Postmodern Condition: A Report on Knowledge," in Cynthia Davison, ed.: *Anytime* (Manchester University Press, Manchester, 1984) p. 215

24 Nicole Stengler: "Leaking Rainbow" in Michael Benedict, ed.: *Cyberspace: First Steps*, p. 57

25 Stephen Hawking: *A Brief History of Time* (Bantam Books, New York, 1998), pp. 106–149

26 *Ibid.*, p. 109

27 Michael Benedict, ed: *Cyberspace: First Steps*, pp. 2, 122

28 Cornell West: "The New Cultural Politics of Difference" in R. Ferguson, M. Gever, T.T. Minh-ha, and C. West, eds.: *Out There: Marginalization and Contemporary Cultures* (MIT Press, Cambridge, MA, 1990), p. 13

29 Paul Virilio: "We May Be Entering an Electronic Gothic Era" in *Architectural Design*, op. cit., p. 57

30 Albert Borgman: *Holding Onto Reality* (University of Chicago Press, 1999), p. 28

31 Henri Lefebvre: *The Production of Space* (Basil Blackwell, Oxford, 1991), p. 62

32 *Ibid.*, p. 10. Substitute information for knowledge and this becomes the substance of the second issue to be discussed here, that of exclusivity.

33 Fred Hoyle: *Frontiers of Astronomy* (Harper and Brothers, New York, 1955)

34 Henri Lefebvre: *op. cit.*, p. 18

35 Robert D. Kaplan, in *The Coming Anarchy* (to be published), predicts that nations, as political entities, will weaken in the twenty-first century, and that by 2100 the global organizing principle will be the city state along with "urban radials of prosperity," that follow major trade routes, much as in the Middle Ages. Alliances between cities will be the new sources of global power, and wars will be fought over bandwidths in cyberspace. Sources of information, rather than territory, will be the social institutions of the future. He calls this "High-tech feudalism."

36 Henri Lefebvre: *op. cit.*, p. 49

37 Edward Soja: *Thirdspace* (Basil Blackwell, Oxford)

38 Alberto Pérez-Gomez and Louise Pelletier: *Architectural Representation and the Perspective Hinge* (MIT Press, Cambridge, MA, and London, 1997), p. 378

39 See Marcos Novak: "Liquid Architecture" in Michael Benedict, *op.cit.*

40 Joseph Weizenbaum: *op. cit*, p. 112

41 John Frazer: *An Evolutionary Architecture* (Architectural Association of London, 1995)

42 Nicholas Negroponte: *The Architecture Machine* (MIT Press, Cambridge, MA, 1970) cited in John Frazer: *An Evolutionary Architecture, ibid.*, p. 18

43 John Frazer: *Ibid.*, p. 24

44 *Ibid.*, p. 99

45 Richard E. Sclove: *Democracy and Technology* (Guilford Press, New York and London, 1995), p. 80

46 Gary Chapman and Joel Yudken: *The 21st Century Project: Setting A New Course for Science and Technology Policy* (Computer Professionals for Social Responsibility, Palo Alto, 1993), p. 102–4

47 Richard E. Sclove: *op. cit.*, p. 40

48 MSM Regional Council, Princeton, and the Regional Plan Association, New York City: "Redesigning the Suburbs: Turning Sprawl into Centers" (Princeton, August 1994)

49 Michael Kwartler: "Regulating the Good You Can't Think Of," *Urban Design International*, 3(1) (1998), p.15

50 *Ibid.*, p. 15

51 Nina Teicholz: "Shaping Cities, Pixels to Bricks: 3-Dimensional Computer Models Make Architects' Ideas Accessible," *New York Times* "Circuits" section, Dec. 16, 1999, D1

52 Michael Sherman of the National Capital Planning Commission reports a great deal of resistance from architects when asked to turn over their three-dimensional files, because they don't want to lose control of the creative process, and the idea of creative ownership, which is behind this resistance, is one barrier to assuming the role of facilitator. It is the

architectural equivalent of the revolution in copyright law now taking place because of the flood of information on the Internet.

53   D.A. Therrien: "Man in the Machine," *Nomad*, No. 4 (1993), pp. 3–4. These mechanisms, Therrien notes, in both cases "allow the few to dominate the many."

54   William Mook: "Techgnosis: Computers as Magic," WELL Conference Proceedings, Jan. 15, 1994, p. 16, and Mark Dery: *Escape Velocity* (Grove Press, New York, 1996), p. 71

55   Thomas Hine: Facing Tomorrow: *What the Future Has Been, What the Future Can Be* (Alfred A. Knopf, New York, 1991), p. 34

56   Nicole Stengler: *op. cit.*, p. 54

57   Robert E. Innis: "Technics and the Bias of Perception," *Philosophy and Social Criticism*, No. 10 (Summer 1984), pp. 67–89. Innis asks if this kind of cognitive focus might tend to elicit fragmented development of perceptual capacities, perhaps with adverse implications for holistic perception, intuition, and synthetic reasoning?

58   Although it is still given a great deal of credence as a traditional view of architectural design in articles such as Denzil Hurley's "About Making" in *Perspective: Yale Architectural Journal*, vol. 19 (1999) there is also an interesting body of ongoing research on the biological connection in architecture, with beginnings in Vitruvius' belief that the proportion of buildings should be based on the human body, continuing on through the Renaissance with Leonardo da Vinci's *Vitruvian Man* with arms and legs extended inside a squared circle and codified in the book *On Growth and Form* by D'Arcy Thompson, first published in 1917, but so influential on late Modernists such as Louis Kahn in its reprinted form. Thompson's thesis has now been extended by George Hersey in *The Monumental Impulse: Architecture's Biological Roots* (MIT Press, Cambridge, MA, 1999), who contends that the human urge to build is instinctive, that "There are genetic homologies between us and other species that build, no matter how distinct from us they seem." Hersey's conclusions, supported by biologist E.O. Wilson at Harvard University, indicate that the human need for permanence may be hardwired into the subconscious of the species.

59   Mark Dery: *Escape Velocity* (Grove Press, New York, 1996), p. 234

60   Ray Kurtzweil: *The Age of the Spritual Machine: When Computers Exceed Human Intelligence* (Viking, New York, 1999)

61   Rob Fixmer: "The Soul of the Next New Machine: Humans (How the Wedding of Brain and Computer Could Change the Universe)," *New York Times*, Nov. 6, 1999, p. A17

62   Karen Hopkin: "Designer Genomes" in *Scientific American*, Dec. 1999, p. 78

63   Starr Roxanne Hiltz and Murray Turoff: *The Network Nation: Human Communication Via Computer* (Addison Wesley, Reading, MA, 1978)

64   Steven Greenhouse: "So Much Work, So Little Time," *New York Times*, Sept. 5, 1999, p. 3

65   Juliet Schor, an economist based at Harvard University, reports higher numbers in her research, of an average increase of 163 hours, or one month of work per year. See Juliet B. Schor: *The Overworked American: The Unexpected Decline of Leisure* (Basic Books, New York, 1999)

66   K.C. Cole: "Time, Space Obsolete in a New View of Universe," *Los Angeles Times*, Nov. 16, 1999, p. A–1. See also: www.superstringtheory.com

Chapter 2

67   http://www.catia.ibm.com/contact/ibmets.html. CATIA stands for Computer Aided Three-dimensional Interactive Application.

68   Karen D. Stein: "Project Diary: Frank Gehry's Dream Project, the Guggenheim Museum Bilbao Draws the World to Spain's Basque Country," *Architectural Record*, 10:97, pp. 75–84

69   Coosje Van Bruggen: *Frank Gehry Guggenheim Museum Bilbao* (Guggenheim Museum Publications, New York, 1997), p. 135

70   Robert McCrum: "The Bilbao Guggenheim," the *Sunday Observer*, 12 Oct. 1997, p. 15–20. See also Thomas Krens, ed.: "Special Issue: Frank Gehry's Guggenheim Museum Bilbao," *Guggenheim Magazine* (Guggenheim Museum Publications, New York, 1997)

71   http:www.detnews.com.

Chapter 3

72   Karl S. Chu: "Genetic Space: Hourglass of the Demiurge," *Architectural Design*, vol. 68, no. 11/12, Nov.–Dec. 1998, p. 69

73   See, for example, the discussion about the emergence of String theory in the introduction (pp.63, 65), which holds that in addition to the three dimensions of space plus one of time described by Einstein, there are seven additional bands, or strings, of energy that combine in an infinite number of permutations to embody the universe. This universe, according to String theorists, is entirely contained in a thin membrane, one of an as yet unknown number of others. Electric, magnetic and nuclear force are believed to be trapped inside our universal membrane, while gravity leaks out, explaining why it is weaker than these other forces.

74   Herbert Muschamp: "An Architect's Moment of Reckoning Arrives," *New York Times*, Sunday, Jan. 30, 2000, pp. 43–44.l. "The European heritage of cultural and scientific knowledge cannot be separated from the will to dominate and exploit non-European civilizations. The museum may be seen as both a mask and an unmasking. It presents the contorted face of classical science to Paris, a city where the history of science has come under close intellectual scrutiny."

75   Herbert Muschamp: "On Staten Island, the New Media Are the Message," *New York Times*, Feb. 27, 2000, p. 52

Chapter 4

76   Joel Kotkin: "Digital City," *Los Angeles Magazine*, July 1997, pp. 94–5

Chapter 5

77   Loukas N. Kalisperis and Randal L. Groninger: "Design Philosophy: Implications for Computer Integration in the Practice of Architecture," in *ACADIA*, 1991, pp. 27–37. In an admitted selection of "notable" firms, nearly 50 percent of interns were CADD proficient, compared to slightly more than 30 percent of architects, 15 percent of managers, and 5 percent of principals.

78   "Digital Worlds," in *Architecture*, June 1997, p. 88

79   Kalisperis and Groninger: *op.cit.*, p. 35

80   Pérez-Gomez and Pelletier: *op.cit*, p. 378

81   "Digital Worlds," *op.cit.*, p. 89

bibliography

Arendt, Hannah: *Crisis of the Republic*
(Harcourt Brace Jovanovich, New York, 1972)

Baudrillard, Jean: *America*
(Verso, New York, 1989)

Baudrillard, Jean: *Simulacres et Simulations*
(Galilee, Paris, 1981)

Bell, Daniel: *The Social Framework of the Information Society*
(MIT Press, Cambridge, MA, 1980)

Bijker, Weibe, E.: *The Social Construction of Technological Systems:
New Directions in the Sociology and History of Technology*
(MIT Press, Cambridge, MA, 1978)

Boole, George: *Laws of Thought: Collected Logical Works*
(Open Court, Chicago, 1940)

Bonner, J.T.: *Morphogenesis*
(Princeton University Press, 1952)

Borgmann, Albert: *Technology and the Character of Contemporary Life:
A Philosophical Inquiry*
(University of Chicago Press, 1984)

Bourdieu, Pierre, and Calman, James, eds: *Social Theory for a Changing
Society* (Westview Press, Boulder, CO, 1991)

Brecher, Jeremy, et al: *Global Visions: Beyond the New World Order*
(South End Press, Boston, 1993)

Burks, A.W.: *Essays on Cellular Automata*
(University of Illinois Press, 1968)

Burnham, Daniel: *The Rise of the Computer State*
(Random House, New York, 1993)

Cairns-Smith, A.G.: *Seven Clues to the Origin of Life*
(Cambridge University Press, 1985)

Chomsky, Noam: *Aspects of the Structure of Syntax*
(MIT Press, Cambridge, MA, 1965)

Chomsky, Noam: *Problems of Knowledge and Freedom*
(Pantheon Books, New York, 1971)

Codd, E.E.: *Cellular Automata*
(Academic Press, New York, 1968)

Davis, L.: *Handbook of Genetic Algorithms*
(Van Nostrand Reinhold, New York, 1991)

Davis, R.: *The Cosmic Blueprint*
(Heinemann, London, 1987)

Dawkins, R.: *The Extended Phenotype*
(Oxford University Press, 1982)

Dennett, D.C.: *Consciousness Explained*
(Penguin Books, London, 1993)

Dreyfus, Hubert L.: *What Computers Can't Do: A Critique of Artificial Reason*
(Harper and Row, New York, 1972)

Dreyfus, Hubert L.: *What Computers Still Can't Do: A Critique of
Artificial Reason*
(MIT Press, Cambridge, MA, 1979)

Dreyfus, Hubert L. and Dreyfus, Stuart: *Mind Over Machine:
The Power of Human Intuitive Expertise in the Era of the Computers*
(Free Press, New York, 1986)

Dulliecco, R.: *The Design of Life*
(Yale University Press, 1987)

DeDuue, C.: *Blueprint for a Cell*
(Patterson Press, 1991)

Eliade, Mircea: *The Sacred and the Profane*
(Harper and Row, New York, 1961)

Feenberg, Andrew: *A Critical Theory of Technology*
(Oxford University Press, 1991)

Forester, T: *High Tech Society: The Story of the Information
Technology Revolution*
(MIT Press, Cambridge, MA, 1987)

Forsyth, R., ed.: *Machine Learning*
(Chapman and Hall, London, 1989)

Frazer, J.H.: "Can Computers be Just a Tool?" in *Systematica: Mutual Uses of Cybernetics and Science*, vol. 8, Amsterdam, 1991, pp. 27–36

Fuller, Buckminster: *Synergetics*
(Macmillan, New York, 1975)

Gertz, Clifford: *The Interpretation of Cultures*
(Basic Books, New York, 1973)

Goldberg, D.E.: *Genetic Algorithms in Search Optimization and Machine Learning*
(Addison Wesley, Reading, MA, 1989)

Hammeroff, S.R.: *Ultimate Computing: Biomolecular Consciousness and Nano-technology*
(Elsevier, 1987)

Heidegger, Martin: *Basic Writings*
(Harper and Row, New York, 1977),
esp. "The End of Philosophy and the Task of Thinking"

Hillier, B. and Hanson, J.: *The Social Logic of Space*
(Cambridge University Press, 1984)

Holland, J.H.: *Adaptation in Natural and Artificial Systems*
(University of Michigan Press, 1975)

Horkheimer, M.: *The Eclipse of Reason*
(Seabury, New York, 1974)

Jones, S.: *The Language of the Genes*
(HarperCollins, 1993)

Jonas, Hans: "Technology and Responsibility: Reflections on the New Tasks of Ethics," in *Social Research*, vol. 40, no. 1, Spring 1973, pp. 31–54

Kaplan, A.: *The Conduct of Inquiry*
(Chandler, San Francisco, 1964)

Kauffman, S.A.: *The Origins of Order: Self Organization and Selection in Evolution*
(Oxford University Press, 1993)

Kegan, Robert: *The Evolving Self: Problem and Process in Human Development*
(Harvard University Press, 1982)

Kettle, S.F.A.: *Symmetry and Structure*
(John Wiley, 1985)

Kidder, Tracy: *Soul of a New Machine*
(Avon Books, New York, 1982)

Koza, J.R.: *Genetic Programming: On the Programming of Computers by Means of Natural Selection*
(MIT Press, Cambridge, MA, 1992)

Kuller, R.: "Architecture and Emotions," in Mikellides, B., ed.: *Architecture for People: Exploration in a New Human Environment*
(Holt, Rinehart and Winston, New York, 1980), pp. 87–100

Lawrence, W.: *Modern Science and Human Values*
(Oxford University Press, 1986)

Lefebvre, H.: *The Production of Space*
(Blackwell, Oxford, 1991)

Levy, S.: *Artificial Life: The Quest for a New Creation*
(Jonathan Cape, London, 1992)

Lifton, R.J.: *The Protean Self: Human Resilience in an Age of Fragmentation*
(Basic Books, New York, 1993)

Luria, A.R.: *Cognitive Development: Its Cultural and Social Foundations*,
ed. M. Cole (Harvard University Press, Cambridge, MA, 1988)

March, L., ed.: *The Architecture of Form*
(Cambridge University Press, 1976)

March, L. and Steadman, P.: *The Geometry of Environment*
(RIBA Publications, London, 1971)

Marshak, A.: *The Roots of Civilization*
(Macmillan, New York, 1972)

Masuda, Y.: *The Information Society as Post Industrial Society*
(World Future Society, Washington, DC, 1981)

Meinhard, H.: *Models of Biological Pattern Formation*
(Academic Press, London, 1982)

Miller, J.: *Living Systems*
(McGraw Hill, New York, 1978)

Mitchell, W.J.: *Computer Aided Architectural Design*
(Van Nostrand Reinhold, New York, 1977)

Mitchell, W.J.: *The Logic of Architecture: Design, Computation and Cognition*
(MIT Press, Cambridge, MA, 1990)

Monad, J.: *Chance and Necessity*
(Collins, London, 1972)

Mosco, V. and Wasko, J., eds: *The Political Economy of Information*
(University of Wisconsin Press, Madison, 1988)

Mumford, L.: *Technics and Civilization*
(Harcourt Brace Jovanovich, New York, 1963)

Mumford, L.: "Authoritarian and Democratic Technics," in *Technology and Culture*, vol. 3, no. 1, Winter, pp. 1–8, 1964

Negroponte, N.: *The Architecture Machine*
(MIT Press, Cambridge, MA, 1970)

Needleman, Carla: *The Work of Craft: An Inquiry in the Nature of Crafts and Craftsmanship*
(Arkana, London, 1986)

Nicholis, G. and Prigogine, J.: *Exploring Complexity*
(Freeman, New York, 1993)

Ornstein, R.E.: *The Psychology of Consciousness*
(W.H. Freeman, San Francisco, 1972)

Pask, G.: *An Approach to Cybernetics*
(Hutchinson, London, 1961)

Pearce, P.: *Structure in Nature as a Strategy for Design*
(MIT Press, Cambridge, MA, 1978)

Penrose, R.: *The Emperor's New Mind: Concerning Computers, Minds and the Laws of Physics*
(Oxford University Press, 1989)

Polanyi, M.: *The Tacit Dimension*
(Doubleday, New York, 1967)

Polanyi, M.: *Personal Knowledge*
(Routledge and Kegan Paul, London, 1971)

Pondsmith, M.: *The View from the Edge: the Cyberpunk Handbook*
(R. Talsortian Games, Berkeley, CA, 1988)

Prigogine, I. and Stengers, I.: *Order Out of Chaos*
(Bantam, New York, 1984)

Pye, D.: *The Nature and Aesthetics of Design*
(Van Nostrand Reinhold, New York, 1982)

Reichardt, J.: *Cybernetic Serendipity*
(Studio Vista, London, 1968)

Rule, J.: *The Politics of Privacy*
(New American Library, New York, 1980)

Schor, J.: *The Overworked American: The Unexpected Decline of Leisure*
(Basic Books, New York, 1999)

Sclove, R. and Scheuer, J.: "The Ghost in the Modem: For Architects of the Information Highway, Some Lessons from the Concrete Interstate," *Washington Post*, 29 May, 1994, p. C3

Sclove, R.: *Democracy and Technology*
(Guilford Press, New York and London, 1995)

233

Seifert, M., Gerbner, G. and Fisher, J., eds: *The Information Gap: How Computers and Other New Communications Technologies Affect Social Distribution of Power*
(Oxford University Press, 1989)

Shweder, R. and LeVine, R.A., eds: *Culture Theory: Essays on Mind, Self and Emotions*
(Cambridge University Press, 1984)

Simon, H.A.: *The Sciences of the Artificial*
(MIT Press, Cambridge, MA, 1969)

Smith, B.R.: *Soft Computing*
(Addison Wesley, Reading, MA, 1984)

Sommer, R.: *Social Design: Creating Buildings with People in Mind*
(Prentice Hall, Englewood Cliffs, NJ, 1983)

Steadman, P.: *The Evolution of Designs: Biological Analogy in Architecture and the Applied Arts*
(Cambridge University Press, 1979)

Stoneman, P.: *Technological Diffusion and the Computer Revolution*
(Cambridge University Press, 1976)

Stonier, T.: *Information and the Internal Structure of the Universe*
(Springer Verlag, 1990)

Sun, M.: "Weighing the Social Costs of Innovation," in *Science*,
30 March 1984, pp. 368–9

Thom, R.: *Structural Stability and Morphogenesis: An Outline of a General Theory of Models*
(Addison Wesley, Reading, MA, 1972)

Thompson, W.D.: *On Growth and Form*
(Cambridge University Press, 1961)

Todd, S. and Latham, W.: *Evolutionary Art and Computers*
(Academic Press, London, 1992)

Tufte, E.R.: *Envisioning Information*
(Graphics Press, Cheshire, CT, 1990)

Turing, A.M.: "Computing Machines and Intelligence," in Ross, S., ed.: *Minds and Machines*
(Prentice Hall, Englewood Cliffs, NJ, 1964)

Turkle, S.: *The Second Self: Computers and the Human Spirit*
(Simon and Schuster, New York, 1984)

Von Neuman, J.: *The Computer and the Brain*
(Yale University Press, New Haven, 1958)

Wad, A.: *Science, Technology and Development*
(Westview Press, Boulder, CO, 1988)

Wagner, R.: *The Invention of Culture*
(University of Chicago Press, 1981)

Wang, H.: *From Mathematics to Philosophy*
(Humanities Press, New York, 1974)

Weizenbaum, J.: *Computer Power and Human Reason: From Judgment to Calculation*
(W.H. Freeman and Co., San Francisco, 1976 and Pelican, London, 1984)

Wittgenstein, L.: *Philosophical Investigations*
(Blackwell, Oxford, 1953)

Wooley, B.: *Virtual Worlds*
(Blackwell, Oxford, 1992)

Yeang, K.: "Bionics: The Use of Biological Analogies for Design,"
in *Architectural Association Quarterly*, no. 4, 1973, pp. 48–57

Yeang, K.: "A Theoretical Framework for Incorporating Ecological Considerations in the Design and Planning of the Built Environment"
(Ph.D. dissertation, Cambridge University, 1981)

Young, J.Z.: *Programs of the Brain*
(Oxford University Press, 1987)

Zuboff, S.: *In the Age of the Smart Machine: The Future of Work and Power*
(Basic Books, New York, 1988)

index

picture credits

The publisher would like to thank the architects and photographers for their kind permission to reproduce images in this book. All images courtesy of the architects, unless indicated below.

© Hélène Binet (116)
© Tom Bonner (166, 170, 171, 174–5, 176, 180, 186–7, 190, 191, 194)
© Naoya Hatakeyama (10, 152 left, 153 right)
© Timothy Hursley (69, 114, 126 right, 128, 131)
© Toyohiko Kobayashi (152, 153 left)
© Susan Oristaglio/Esto (97 right)
© Markus Pillhofer (118)
  Courtesy James Steele (18 right, 22, 23, 25 left, 112, 113)
© VIEW/Peter Cook (104 left)
  Brandon Welling (95)
© Gerald Zugmann (15, 117)

author's acknowledgements

Laurence King and John Stoddart at Calmann and King were instrumental in initially supporting the idea behind this project and commissioning editor Philip Cooper and editor Liz Faber have tirelessly seen it through from the beginning. Their enthusiasm, continual support and patience while it has evolved have made it possible for me to include new work in this fast breaking field.

My gratitude also to all those who have contributed. In the order that they appear here, they are: Jon Jerde and Albert Vaas, Anne Matranga and Ralph Yanaga of the Jerde Partnership, Michael Hsu of Softmirage, John Frazer, Michael Kwartler of the Environmental Simulation Center, Stephan Behnisch and Christof Jantzen of Behnisch, Behnisch and Partner, Joey Myers, Jonathan Ward, Hin Ah Park and Peter Pran at NBBJ, Michael Rotondi, Clarke Stevens and Mary Beth Leonard at RoTo, Thom Mayne, John Endicott and Elizabeth Meyer of Morphosis, James Stewart Polshek, Todd Schliemann and Susan Strauss at James Stewart Polshek and Partners, and Holly Evarts of the Hayden Planetarium, New York City, Sir Norman Foster, David Jenkins and Katy Harris of Sir Norman Foster and Partners, Nicholas Grimshaw and Romaine Govett at Nicholas Grimshaw and Partners, Cesar Pelli and Mig Halprin at Cesar Pelli Associates, Abdel Wahed El Wakil, Kisho Kurokawa and Yoshiko Takanawa of Kisho Kurokawa Architect and Associates, Arata Isozaki of Arata Isozaki Architect, Wolf Prix of Coop Himmelb(l)au, Frank Gehry, Edwin Chan and Keith Mendenhall of Frank O. Gehry and Associates, Joel Rosenbaum of BEI Associates, Sherry Chow of Dassault Systems of America, Karl Chu, Toyo Ito and Mariko Nishimura of Toyo Ito and Associates, Lars Spuybrock of NOX, Ken Yeang at T.F. Hamzah and Yeang SDN.BHD, Peter Eisenman and Sebastian Mittendorfer at Eisenman Architects, Eric Owen Moss, Ray Ricord and Jennifer Leung of Eric Owen Mass, James O'Conner and Tony Tran at Moore, Ruble, Yudell, Janet Stephansen of Arup and Partners, Los Angeles and Dean Robert Timme, Douglas Noble, Karen Kensek, Clayton An, Melanie Beisswenger, Tommy Chan, Calvin Kam, Jia Geng, Madhu Gupta, Keith Ireland, Stacy Lin, Tami Nguyen, Chris State, Daniel Yang, Satoko Yokori and Franco Wu Fang at the University of Southern California.

Thanks also to: Yuwen Peng, Elizabeth Valmont, Grace Kim, Odile Fillion, Marilyn Tullius, and especially to my son Christopher, for suggesting key references at important points during the development of the text, and to Angelica de Jesus for all her help.

James Steele

First published in 2002 in the United States by
Watson-Guptill Publications
a division of BPI Communications, Inc.
770 Broadway, New York, NY 10003
www.watsonguptill.com

Published in 2001 by Laurence King Publishing
an imprint of Calmann & King Ltd
71 Great Russell Street
London WC1B 3BP
Copyright © 2001 James Steele
Copyright in the design © 2001 Calmann & King Ltd

Library of Congress Cataloging-in-Publication Data for this title can
be obtained by writing to the Library of Congress, Washington D.C.

ISBN 0-8230-0324-8

Designed by state

Printed in Hong Kong

1 2 3 4 5 6 7 8 9 10 / 10 09 08 07 06 05 04 03 02